BREAKING OPEN THE CREEDS

What Can They Mean for Christians Today?

Richard W. Kropf

Paulist Press
New York/Mahwah, NJ

Printed with Ecclesiastical Permission.
+ Most Reverend Earl Boyea, Bishop of Lansing.
February 22, 2009, the Feast of the Chair of St. Peter

Cover design by Sharyn Banks
Book design by Lynn Else

Library of Congress Cataloging-in-Publication Data

Kropf, Richard W., 1932–
    Breaking open the creeds : what can they mean for Christians today? /Richard W. Kropf.
        p. cm.
    Includes bibliographical references (p.   ) and index.
    ISBN 978-0-8091-4550-8 (alk. paper)
    1. Apostles' Creed. 2. Nicene Creed. 3. Creeds—History and criticism. I. Title.
    BT993.3.K76 2011
    238´.11—dc22

                                                              2010026602

Published by Paulist Press
997 Macarthur Boulevard
Mahwah, New Jersey 07430

www.paulistpress.com

Printed and bound in the
United States of America

CONTENTS

We…should…with perseverance keep running in the race which lies ahead of us. Let us keep our eyes fixed on Jesus, who leads us in our faith and brings it to perfection.

(Heb 12:1b–2a, NJB)

ACKNOWLEDGMENTS

I wish to thank the Most Rev. Patrick R. Cooney, bishop of Gaylord, Michigan, for his encouragement and guidance in what began mostly as a personal journey into the past to explore the riches of the Christian tradition. Thanks also to Rev. Lawrence Boadt, CSP, president and publisher of Paulist Press, who saw the possibilities of turning my efforts into something that might provide not only Catholics but other Christians who take these creeds seriously with the opportunity to share these explorations. Thanks are also due to Dr. Rudolph Goetz, Bill Panagos, Patrick Stonehouse, Krinne Walsh, Charlene Ford, and others who expressed their interest, advice, and support. Thanks also to Vicki Looker for her assistance and to Nancy de Flon of Paulist Press for her suggestions and work in preparing the manuscript for publication. Although this book was conceived as an ecumenical exploration into the creeds, special recognition is also due to the Most Rev. Carl F. Mengeling, the bishop of Lansing, and his successor, the Most Rev. Earl A. Boyea, who as my ecclesiastical superior and with the advice of his theological advisor, Msgr. Robert D. Lunsford, gave his approval for the publication of this book for its use in specifically Catholic study groups. All biblical quotations, unless otherwise noted, are taken from the New Revised Standard Version translation. Translations from the writings of St. Cyril of Jerusalem are those provided by the International Committee for English in the Liturgy. Unless otherwise noted, the translation of the Creed of Nicaea-Constantinople used here is the ecumenical text issued in 1988 by the English Language Liturgical Consultation.

INTRODUCTION

What do we mean—indeed, what *can* we mean—when, during our worship, we dutifully recite the hallowed words of the formal Christian Creeds? Are we doing this simply for tradition's sake—or can they really be meaningful for Christians today?

To answer these questions and the challenges they present, we have to keep a number of things in mind.

First, these creeds are very old. The Apostles' Creed is the Roman version of a second-century baptismal profession of faith similar to those found all around the early Christian world. The Nicene Creed, which gets its name from the Council of Nicaea held in AD 325, was based on one of the ancient baptismal creeds, and even then it was not completed until the First Council of Constantinople was held in 381.

As for the purpose of the creeds, St. Cyril of Jerusalem, one of the bishops who attended the First Council of Constantinople, tells his flock:

> This summary of the faith was not composed at man's whim; the most important sections were chosen from the whole Scripture to constitute and complete a comprehensive statement of the faith. Just as the mustard seed contains in a small grain many branches, so this brief statement of the faith keeps in its heart, as it were, all the religious truth to be found in Old and New Testament alike. That is why, my brothers, you must conserve and preserve the traditions you are now receiving. Inscribe them across your heart.[1]

While much of the phrasing of these creeds was adopted from the scriptures, the final decision as to what books should be included in the New Testament was, to a large extent, determined by the content of these creeds. Nothing contrary to the agreed-upon tradition—such as the Gnostic-oriented *Gospel of Thomas* or the *Gospel of Judas*, both of which either denied or downgraded the humanity of Jesus—was admitted to the canon or official list. Thus the relationship between the Apostles' and Nicene Creeds and the scriptures appears to be deeply intertwined, almost to the extent that their authority depends on each other.

For that reason alone, the importance of these creeds cannot be overstated. Later creeds, such as Pope Paul VI's 1968 "Credo of the People of God," or the many other teachings of ecumenical councils and confessional statements of the various Christian denominations down through the ages, may have added further clarifications, yet, none has been as constitutive of Christian beliefs as these two time-honored creeds. In addition, in ecumenical circles it is generally held that these creeds form the foundation of any future doctrinal agreement.

As we shall soon see, however, advances in scientific knowledge have brought about major changes in our understanding of the universe. Thus, if we are to extract the meaning of these ancient creedal formulas for our faith, we must to some extent reinterpret them, if not reformulate them, so that they make sense to us today.

In Latin the traditional name for an official profession of faith, or a creed, is *symbolum*. The dictionary meaning of *symbol*—from the Greek *sym* (= "together") and *ballo* (= "to place" or "to throw")—is "a token or pledge by which one infers a thing." This may indeed be the way we understand the function of the creeds today: that they have functioned, first of all, as *professions* of faith, whether it be in an individual form ("I believe") or collective form ("We believe"—used originally at Nicaea, then later changed to the singular at Constantinople). However, according to the ancient meaning of the term, the creeds are also *symbols* because they are, as Cyril said, a summary in which the various beliefs have been brought together; in the case of Nicaea, they are also the result of a coming together or meeting of minds by those charged with the task of teaching the Christian faith—hence, as we might say today, a consensus statement.

Nevertheless, *profession* is an especially evocative word, especially in this context. It means, first of all, a "declaration." But its roots are in the Latin words *pro*, meaning "for," and *fateri*, meaning "to take a vow" and thus committing oneself to do something for the sake of something or someone greater than oneself. Hence, the second major meaning of *profession* is a vocation or occupation requiring advanced training and a high degree of dedication, such as a life given over to the practice of medicine, teaching, or the law—or, in the case of a religious profession, to God. It is a life that, if truly lived in a professional manner, is given over to the pursuit of an ideal.

So it is with faith. Faith is not a thing but an action. Through it we are in the process of trying to reach God. We are attempting to reach out beyond ourselves and beyond our narrow and all-too-often self-centered world. This means that we are taking a risk, betting the meaning of our life on something totally beyond us, something that we do not yet see clearly. Thus we outdo ourselves, over and over again, like a potential Olympic athlete, trying to reach the ideal we have yet to achieve, convinced that if we keep trying hard enough, we will eventually reach our goal. As the apostle Paul put it, we must "run so as to win it" (1 Cor 9:24), not because we clearly see it yet, but because we have been promised it nonetheless. But even if we do not always run as fast as we should, nevertheless, "we walk by faith and not by sight" (2 Cor 5:7).

This should tell us something else of great importance. Since the middle of the nineteenth century, scholars of religion and of the Bible have increasingly distinguished between the historical Jesus, or "the Jesus of history," as distinguished from "the Christ of faith." The Jesus of history is derived from what little historically verified information we have of the man Jesus of Nazareth that can be gleaned from the data in the Gospels and other writings of the period. The Christ of faith is the glorified Jesus—Jesus Christ risen from the dead and proclaimed as Lord, the Son of God; indeed, as God's own Word made flesh.

So we may well ask, how did we get from there to here, from history to belief, from "the Son of Man" to "the Son of God," much less to "true God from true God"? And even more, we must ask, how do we make this leap of faith today? This is the challenge of the creeds, and to understand this challenge is to try to understand the very dynamic of faith.

Admittedly, for many, such a leap is not easily understood. The popular Christian apologist C. S. Lewis once likened faith to the process of children's playacting, which may seem like pure make-believe to adults, but which in reality is a very serious business, a very necessary preliminary step to taking on adult roles and responsibilities in life. In professing our faith in what we cannot yet see, said Lewis, we are in the process of evolving to a higher stage of humanity by practicing to become what we not yet are, but someday may be.

However, to take Lewis's analogy one step further, could it not be applied to the life of Jesus himself? Humanly speaking, Jesus of Nazareth appears, from gospel accounts, to have acted on the conviction that he was God's promised Messiah, the one whom the prophet Daniel called "the Son of Man." Yet most of the time, rather than *proclaiming* this openly, Jesus instead *acted out*, in his own life of preaching and ministry, what he believed the new era of God's kingdom on earth would be. But he also freely underwent death, apparently believing that the reality of his messiahship and the future kingdom of God could be made evident only through his resurrection from the dead. And so it was, to those who believed in him—even to the point where the Son of Man became recognized as the Son of God, as was to be proclaimed in the New Testament and the creeds.

But is all of this believable to us today? The answer depends on what you believe is to be the future fate of humankind. So here we might introduce a comparison.

Back in 1768, Voltaire—a deist who was skeptical of all organized religion—famously wrote: "If God did not exist, it would be necessary to invent him." Yet, if anything, our increasing awareness of the *past* history of the universe inclines us, perhaps more than ever, to question the mysterious origins of all existence—even if creation did not take place in quite the naive manner we once imagined. If Voltaire's ironic observation was correct over two centuries ago, how much more it is true today!

On the other hand, we are increasingly aware of the *future* of the universe, which, if we can believe the scientists, is limited—even if the scale and timetable are less immediate than thought to be in Jesus' own time. Yet perhaps, even more than in Jesus' day, this increased awareness should drive us, if we are to be persons of faith, toward a hope in our redemption and a belief in a Savior to rescue us from this delayed but increasingly certain fate.

We also sense that such a salvation, which is a share in God's own eternal life, can be revealed only through someone who was fully in possession of divine life. In other words, to paraphrase Voltaire, if there were no Christ, we should have to invent one. But we don't have to, because here is where faith has already taken us one step further. We believe we have already found him, the Christ, in the person of Jesus. If not Jesus, once the job description is fully understood, can anyone suggest a plausible substitute?

Finally, to round the picture out, we believe that through the same divine Spirit that made Jesus God's own Son, we too are made sons and daughters of God. As the early Church theologians repeatedly said: "God became man so that man might become God." So in our recitation of the creeds, we are merely connecting the dots so to speak, making the connections in our minds that we are called to live out in the daily living of our lives.

However, it is my conviction that we must do more than simply connect the dots. Mindful of Socrates' dictum that "the unexamined life is not worth living," this little commentary has been written with a new sense of urgency in mind, in the conviction that without constantly questioning and reexamining our beliefs, our understanding of our faith cannot possibly grow as it should, especially if we are, as St. Peter enjoins us, "to be ready to give an account for the hope that is in you" (1 Pet 3:15).

If the results of this effort seem much less venturesome than some of my previous efforts, it must nevertheless be understood that the task of a theologian is twofold. Like the scribe described in the Gospel of Matthew (13:52), the challenge is not only to explore new ways of understanding God and his ways—a task on which I have spent a great deal of time in past years—but also to shed new light on the old ways as well. Either task, taken by itself, is relatively easy. The real challenge, as I have undertaken in this short attempt, is to explore new ways of reconciling the two.

Richard W. Kropf
Montmorency County, Michigan
January 2009

THE CREEDS AND THE CATECHISM

Following is a list, arranged according to the chapters in this book, of the sections in the *Catechism of the Catholic Church* that discuss Church teachings related to that chapter. It is by no means an exhaustive list; additional references can be found in the general index in the back of the *Catechism*. The numbers after the chapter title refer to the paragraph numbers in the second edition of the *Catechism*, which are printed in bold at the start of each paragraph.

For a general introduction to the creeds and to the Nicene and Apostles' Creeds in particular, see paragraphs no. 185–97.

1. One God: 200–202
2. The Father Almighty: 268–78
3. Creator of All Things: 325–27, 337–38
4. God's Only Son: 422–24, 441–51
5. True God from True God: 464–69
6. One in Being: 242, 262
7. Born of the Virgin Mary: 484–511
8. Crucified: 595–600, 624–30
9. Risen from the Dead: 638–44
10. Ascended into Heaven: 659–67
11. He Will Come Again: 668–82
12. The Holy Spirit: 683–88
13. The Holy Catholic Church: one, 813–22; holy, 823–29; catholic, 830–56; apostolic, 857–65
14. The Communion of Saints: 946–62
15. Baptism and Forgiveness: 1262–66
16. Resurrection and Life Everlasting: 988–1004

Anyone wishing to explore the creeds in the context of their ecumenical dimension should consult the World Council of Churches document:

http://www.oikoumene.org/en/resources/documents/wcc-commissions/faith-and-order-commission/iii-apostolic-faith/towards-sharing-the-one-faith/towards-sharing-the-one-faith.html.

Part I

God as Creator

ORDER O~

I OF FAITH

ly, the profession of
lebrations. ~

We believe in one G~
the Father, the Almigh~
maker of heaven and earth,
of all that is seen and unseen.

We believe in one Lord, Jesus Chr~
the only Son of God,
eternally begotten of the F~
God from God, Light ~
true God from tru~
begotten, not ma~
Through him ~
For us m~
he car~

~ll how d~

y t~
h~

ONE GOD

I believe in God.
(Apostles' Creed)

We believe in one God.
(Nicene Creed)

Most people, when queried by pollsters, say that they believe in God. But do they really *believe*? It seems that for most people the existence of a god, a "first cause," a "prime (or unmoved) mover" (Aristotle), or an "uncaused cause" (Aquinas) is simply a matter of logic and not of belief—if by belief you mean taking someone else's word for it. For many, it is simply a matter of trying to account logically for the existence of anything at all, particularly once one becomes aware of the fact that everything in this world—most certainly ourselves, and most likely the whole universe—is impermanent. For others, it may be the result of contemplation or appreciation of the intricacy and beauty of the universe. Either way, on this level, which one might call philosophical—but which we also might simply call common sense—whether one names this preexisting being the "Force" (as in *Star Wars*) or pure boundless "Creativity" (as has one contemporary theologian), it seems that for most people belief in God is primarily a matter of using pure reason or even just one's intuition.

At the same time, on this same philosophical or logical level, we have to affirm that God is *one*—otherwise God cannot be truly God in the full sense of that word: the "uncaused cause" that is the origin of *everything* else that has existence. Thus Christianity, like Judaism before it, teaches that there is only one God—and hence is uncompromisingly monotheistic.

This was not always clear to people in the ancient world. When Moses was confronted by the burning bush in the desert, he asked God for his name, which God revealed in the mysterious word *Yahweh*, which seems almost impossible to translate but comes out something like "I am." This seems to imply that this God is the only God who really exists, or at the very least, the only one that counts. Yet, as we can see from the first commandment, the impression remained that there were other gods. In fact, after it became the custom, by the time of Jesus, never to pronounce that most sacred name of Yahweh out of fear of its profanation, Jews often reverted to using the generic word for God, which is a plural form. Thus the word *Elohim*— which literally translates into "gods"—might be seen today as the equivalent of the more abstract term *divinity*. Another way of avoiding the pronunciation of Yahweh was to substitute the term *Adonai*, or "Lord." Later on, in order to remind the Jews of this custom, rabbis and scribes had the vowel marks (a later addition to Hebrew texts) of one or the other of these two substitutes written under the original consonants for the most sacred name. This, in turn, resulted in the misunderstanding among non-Jews that the Old Testament name of God was *Jehovah*—a word that, in Hebrew, doesn't exist!

Today, however, the real problem that many people have is not what name to use, but whether or not God even exists. For some, *God* is just a shorthand term for whatever *is*. They are, at least in a loose sense of the word, pantheists, meaning they believe that everything is God. These persons, who apparently believe that the universe in some form or another has always existed and always will, say they see no need for anything like a personal God. Others, seeing all the suffering and evil in the universe, have concluded that if there is anything like a God that is responsible for all this, they don't want to have anything to do with him. (We'll get back to that problem soon.)

At the root of all these problems, it seems, is a widespread confusion over just what the word *God* really means. For many philosophers and theologians, the term really means the source or "ground" of all existence; as St. Augustine put it, God is "Being in itself." The great medieval mystic Meister Eckhart went so far as to say that everything, insofar as it shares God's existence, is God! Put that way, one can understand why Eckhart was accused of being a pantheist. But his point was to stress that we are all living only a borrowed existence. Anyone who imagines that he or she, or even the whole world, exists in its own right, apart from the God who sustains all things in being, is living in a state of self-delusion— something like imagining that one can rise above the earth (as our ancestors used to put it) by pulling up on one's own bootstraps. But if nothing else, it is clear from such philosophical and theological reflections that God is something far beyond our childhood image of an old man with a long white beard living somewhere off in space.

Speaking seriously, however, where do such images come from? Sigmund Freud, the great pioneer of modern psychiatry, saw the obvious connection between our image of God and our image of our own human fathers. But it does not take any great genius to see that if the Bible itself (in Gen 1:26) says that humans are made in God's image and likeness, then, having such an exalted opinion of ourselves, we will return the compliment but all too often it is in the form of a distorted image of ourselves. This is certainly a problem, as we shall see when we get to the next phrase in the creeds.

Philosophers and theologians, and especially the great mystics, have from time to time reminded us that there are, essentially, two ways of approaching the subject of trying to imagine what or who God really is. The first way is to picture what is the greatest, the most sublime, the most perfect, the most of whatever you can think of, and then conclude that whatever God is, God is even more than that. This is what is sometimes called positive theology, or the way of analogy, which is to say we liken God to something else but then finally have to admit that the comparison falls far short of what we are trying to say.

The second way, the way of negative theology, is just the opposite and asks: If every analogy or comparison eventually breaks down, then why attempt it in the first place? Instead, why not simply admit that the ultimate ground or basis of our existence is utterly beyond us, even while it is present in the very depths of our being? This is not to say that we cannot be in touch with that mysterious presence. In fact, being or living in the awareness of that presence is probably the touchstone of, or the highway to, all true spirituality. But we should not fool ourselves that, even in that awareness, we will end up knowing all the answers, or even just the beginning of a few of them.

Finally, perhaps a few words about still another way that we might experience or think about God. We all seek *meaning* or purpose in our lives. Certainly many books have been written on that subject—which would seem to indicate that this is a major human preoccupation. Quite a few of these books, however, especially those written by such modern existentialist philosophers as Jean-Paul Sartre, Albert Camus, and others, have concluded that there is no meaning or purpose in the universe other than that which we ourselves supply in our own minds. That seems, to say the least, rather egocentric. It supposes that this vast universe, which science tells us existed at least thirteen billion years before humans appeared on the face of the earth, was, for all that time, essentially meaningless and without purpose. Of course, one might suppose life exists or will exist on other planets, life that might define its own meaning. But the universe seems too vast, too mysterious, and too utterly mind-boggling to suppose that the purpose or meaning of it all is just something we make up for ourselves. There is a great deal more to it than that. In other words, for many people God is not only what gives meaning to the existence of the universe; God is *that ultimate meaning* in itself. All the rest is just commentary—and that includes even our own existence!

QUESTIONS FOR REFLECTION AND DISCUSSION

1. What do you see as the greatest influence on your own belief in God?
2. How do you imagine God in your own mind?
3. What most threatens your own belief in God?
4. How do you deal with that threat?

THE FATHER ALMIGHTY

I believe in God, the Father almighty.
(Apostles' Creed)

We believe in one God, the Father, the Almighty.
(Nicene Creed)

We have already seen how, in their efforts to protect the sanctity of God's holy name, Jews eventually referred to God in the rather general term *Elohim*. One other common way of addressing God, especially in prayer, was *Lord* or, in Hebrew, *Adonai*.

All these attempts to protect the sanctity and the transcendent otherness of God's name only highlight what is so radical and distinct about Jesus' own experience of God and his insistence on calling God *Abba*, or Father. This also raises the challenge and the problems it presents for his followers today—especially for those who see in this practice more than a vestige of sexism. But in dealing with this issue of sexism, we should remember several things.

First, we are dealing here with symbols or analogies; that is, we are speaking of that which is, in a very real sense, incomprehensible—something that is, to a large extent, almost totally beyond our grasp. God, as such, is beyond such created categories as gender or sex. Yet as Creator, God exhibits certain qualities that may remind us of a loving, caring parent or guardian, or still yet, a benevolent ruler or king.

Cataphatic / apophatic

Second, at the time the creeds were composed, indeed in the days when the various books of the Bible were written, the understanding of biology was not what it is today. Back then, it was believed that only males actually transmitted life. Females, on the other hand, nourished it. If a child looked more like the mother than the father, it was only because she was like the soil or earth in which the seed took root and grew. Of course, today we know better. A mother shares her genetic makeup with her offspring just as much as any father does. And in the normal course of things, she generally shares much more. Which parent the child resembles we now know has to do with which genes are more dominant as well as with the random combinations of DNA.

Third, in many other religions we find references to God—or, in the case of polytheistic religions, the chief god— as being the "Father of the gods," often in tandem with the earth as our "Mother." Because of this, a Jew would never think of addressing God as Mother—even if for no other reason than this would be the first step back into the sin of *idolatry*. That would be making a god or goddess out of something created, thus mistaking a mere creature in place of the Creator.

Today, however, except for a small group of environmentalists who seem bent on reviving the old pagan worship of Mother Nature, or *Gaia* as some prefer to call her, the most common form of idolatry that we see in the world today is not the worship of nature as such, but instead the worship of ourselves and our own accomplishments and pleasures. It may not be in the form of bowing down before things or offering up incense before a picture or statue of the emperor or king, as the early Christians were forced to do. But suppose we simply ask what most occupies our thoughts, worries, and hopes—or maybe more to the point, how we spend our weekends, especially our Sunday mornings. In other words, what comes first in our lives? As Jesus reminded us, "You cannot serve both God and wealth" (Matt 6:24).

So why do we persist in worshiping or serving these other false gods or goals in life rather than the true God? Perhaps it is because of two things. For one, God seems so remote and far-off for many people, or maybe, from another perspective, too deep a subject. We humans, while we may be rational animals, as the philosopher says, are animals nonetheless, and are thus prone to live on the superficial, sensory level. We are attracted to baubles, trinkets, and curiosities.

Even if we go beyond these superficialities to a much deeper level, we worry too much about our own security. This, too, is natural. If people tend to be concerned about what they have to eat, what they have to wear, or where they live, it is probably because they have, in a way, inherited these concerns from ancestors who could not always be sure where their next meal was coming from or whether they actually would have a place to live. But for most of us today, should these things be a real concern—at least if we live in what we like to call civilization? One would hardly think so. But what this all comes down to is having a sense of security.

This search for security in turn takes us directly back to the issue of faith, because faith, at its heart, implies—in fact, means in the gospel sense of the word—a loving trust in God. So while we may indeed say, "We believe in God," we really lack faith unless we truly trust in God as we would a loving, caring Father.

Instead, if we are truly followers of Jesus, we will imitate him by calling upon his—as well as *our*—Father, not as terrified subjects or slaves of some despotic earthly tyrant, but rather as children confident that our heavenly Father, who provides food for "the birds of the air" or who "clothes the grass of the field," will give us whatever we need (Matt 6:27–33).

This brings us to still another aspect of these two creeds: in the same breath in which we call God our Father, both creeds say that this same God is also the Almighty (*El Shaddai* in Hebrew)—in other words, all-powerful, or omnipotent. If that is the case, and God is supposedly good, how do we account for all the pain and suffering, as well as the outright evil that we find in the universe? How can God really be so loving and *good*? This problem not only bothered ancient thinkers, such as the author of the Book of Job in the Old Testament, but contemporary thinkers as well, especially after such twentieth-century disasters as the great World Wars and the Holocaust.

One solution to this problem that seemed to work, at least for a time, was to blame all evil and suffering on humans, or at least on the first humans who succumbed to the temptation proposed by Satan or the devil. According to this solution, known as *original sin*, sin—whether that of humans or even of angels (at least the ones who turned into devils)—came first, and death and all the other evils followed. Such a solution even seemed to make sense, although it was hard to understand how a God who supposedly knows everything wasn't responsible for these disasters as well. In some civilizations the solution was to blame all this on another god, an evil god. (In fact, many scripture scholars today see the story in the Book of Genesis as being a variation of the old "good god versus bad god" theology of the ancient Babylonians.)

Let us go back to the understanding of God as Father or a loving parent. We need only to think of what good and far-seeing parents do. They provide and, to the best of their ability, they protect. But they also know that they must not be overprotective, lest their children never be able to grow up to be mature, responsible persons capable of life on their own. Not that we can ever be completely independent of God—apart from God, nothing can exist! But as the Bible tells us, God wished to create us in his own image and likeness, and if that phrase means anything at all, it means that God has given us the power, to a large extent, for better or for worse, to decide our own fate.

QUESTIONS FOR REFLECTION AND DISCUSSION

1. How essential to Christianity is Jesus' own characterization of God as *Abba*, or Father? How should it be understood today?

2. Do you see any danger to Christianity in the revival of the ancient concept of Gaia or Mother Earth?

3. To what extent do you see belief in divine providence as being essential to Christian belief?

4. Do you consider the idea of original sin as an adequate explanation for evil in the world? Why or why not?

CREATOR OF ALL THINGS

...creator of heaven and earth...
(Apostles' Creed)

...maker of heaven and earth, of all that is, seen and unseen...
(Nicene Creed)

While this later addition to the earliest versions of the baptismal creed speaks of God as the Creator (in Latin, *creatorem*) of heaven and earth, the Nicene Creed instead uses the more common word *maker* (in Latin, *factorem*) and then specifies "of all that is, seen and unseen." Is there a reason for the difference? To *create* means to make something out of nothing. In the first chapter of Genesis, however, even where a special Hebrew verb (*bara*) is used, this is not clear. In fact, in speaking of what came before creation as *tohu w'bohu* (translated as "a formless void" in the New Revised Standard Version, and in the Jerusalem Bible as "trackless waste and emptiness"), Genesis gives the impression that God was working with primeval matter. In fact, the only mention of creation from nothing in biblical literature comes in the Second Book of Maccabees (7:28), but even that seems contradicted by the Book of Wisdom's use of "created...from formless matter" (11:17), recalling Genesis. Perhaps this is why the Council of Nicaea chose the more common term *maker*—to emphasize that whatever came first was also God's work. In other words, God is the cause of *everything* that exists.

"Everything" is immensely more than the writers of the Bible or the creeds could have ever imagined. Today, astronomers have determined that only about 4 percent of the universe is composed of the visible matter that makes up stars, planets, and ourselves. Yet the effects of gravitational attraction lead them to conclude that the rest must consist of what they call invisible "dark matter" and, even more, of a "dark energy" that is causing the expansion of the universe not only to continue, but even, according to the latest findings, to be speeding up!

By the time the creeds were formulated, most educated people no longer thought the earth was flat, with the sky stretched out overhead like an overturned bowl as described in the Bible. But it was not until the priest and mathematician Nicholas Copernicus suggested that the earth revolved around the sun, and some years later Galileo proved it with his telescope, that we began to realize we are not living in the center of the universe. Not only that, but in the last century we learned that even the Milky Way, the galaxy in which the sun and our planet is located, is only one of about one and a quarter billion or so galaxies in the visible universe. Now, given the fact that most of these galaxies contain somewhere between 100 billion and 200 billion stars, this means there could be as many as one sextillion planets in the universe (a sextillion is 10 with twenty zeros after it). That does not mean all of them are suitable for life like our planet, but even if only a very small proportion of them have favorable conditions for life, then there is an overwhelming probability that we are not alone in this vast universe. Certainly, for most people all this seems too much to comprehend, or if they try to, it seems to challenge traditional ideas of creation and the Creator.

The first thing we must remember is that this part of the creeds is not about *how* God created everything, but about *the fact that* God is the origin or first cause of everything without exception. If this is the case, it seems odd that so many believers seem threatened by the idea of evolution. But the Catholic response to all this is clear. Just like Copernicus, who inspired Galileo, another priest-scientist, Georges Lemaître, was among those who first proposed what is now called (at first rather derisively but now generally accepted) the big bang theory. If so, Christians should take science, including evolutionary science, seriously. As Pope John Paul II said, "Evolution is more than a hypothesis"—in other words, more than just a theory. It is probably the only comprehensive and, one might add, comprehensible way of understanding the development of our universe. Still, reason tells us that you can't get anything, even a big bang, from absolutely nothing. This is where faith alone provides a plausible answer as to *why* it all began or why anything exists to begin with.

This is also where an understanding of creation as taking place through the evolution of the universe, and especially through the evolution of life on this planet, helps explain, as Darwin pointed out, the existence of so much suffering and apparent evil as well. For if we understand the beginnings of the universe as being something like the chaotic state of the big bang or like the formless matter described in Genesis, then we also have to understand that we have evolved as free creatures from a universe in which chance or random events are inevitable. In other words, freedom cannot arise from a world of clockwork-like certainty. In a world where everything would have turned out just as God had "planned," we humans would have turned out to be robots! Obviously, this is not the case. Nor would it seem to be what God really wanted.

This new evolutionary understanding of the origins of suffering, death, and other evils gives a new and more plausible meaning to a very puzzling passage in holy scripture. St. Paul tells us that "creation has been subjected to futility" and is in "bondage to decay" (see Rom 8:20–21). Knowing what we now know about the vastness of the universe, ascribing this futility or decay—or, perhaps better, entropy—to an original sin seems rather implausible. But when seen as a basic and necessary condition of creation, this new view of the origins of what we take to be evil in the universe gives a whole new cosmic dimension—far beyond what Paul could have possibly imagined—to the story of redemption that is to follow. It also teaches us that just as creation is an ongoing process, so too God's revelation to us continues the more we learn about and reflect upon God's workings in this evolving universe.

Finally, we must ask about the issue of *intelligent design* that has been so much in the news these recent years. Believers in *theistic evolution*—that is, the idea that God has used evolution to create—have no problem with the idea that God in some sense designed the whole process. They do, however, have a problem with the idea that God has to keep intervening or interfering with the detailed workings of this process from time to time to keep it on track. If that really were the case, it would seem to picture God as a not-so-intelligent designer who had to keep correcting his mistakes! Furthermore, knowing what we now do about human origins and our inherited tendencies toward subhuman behavior, it would seem that God might have done somewhat better if he had intervened in a special way to create a more suitable home for the immortal soul. Indeed, in his 1950 encyclical *Humani Generis*, Pope Pius XII admitted that it could very well be that, at least physically speaking, the human species evolved from other forms of life. He only insisted that the human soul be seen as the special creation of God. More recently, Pope John Paul II repeated this same viewpoint, yet at the same time admitted in his encyclical *Evangelium Vitae* (*The Gospel of Life*, 60 and 61)[2] that we do not know exactly when this special creation of the human soul takes place in the course of human development.

This lack of certainty only reinforces the Church's insistence on the sanctity and inviolability of human life at all stages of development, from the first moment of conception to the final moment of death. It further underscores the idea that creation is not an event that took place eons ago, but something that still continues today as an ongoing process, and that creation and procreation are closely linked. Although we may trace the physical beginnings of the universe back some 13.7 billion years ago to a big bang, God's creative activity continues. God is not only the Creator, but also the Sustainer of the whole universe. Too often God is still pictured as a remote or abstract Architect of a clockwork-like universe. This view grew out of the seventeenth-century mathematical theories of Sir Isaac Newton, which were suitable for that time and which still operate even within the scale of interplanetary space. But in the end, as the confirmation of Einstein's relativistic physics have proved, the older, more mechanistic concepts of nature have proved inadequate in the total cosmic framework. Something conceptually much bolder is needed. As Albert Einstein put it, "I want to know what God himself was thinking."

In much the same way, we need to undergo a major shift or upheaval in our ideas about God. We need to put away, as St. Paul says, our "childish ways" (1 Cor 13:11) to be fed with the "solid food" (1 Cor 3:2) of mature thinking. Not only do we have to give up the idea that creation happened long ago (whether it be 13.7 billion years ago according to the scientists, or only 6,800 years ago according to the fundamentalists), but even more, we need to let go of the notion of a God who is far from us, beyond the boundaries of space and time. Instead, we must realize that creation is a process that is still continuing, and while it is true that God is far beyond us in the sense of *transcending* all creation, God as the foundation or ground of all that exists is also *immanent* within this ongoing process.

There is no place on earth or in this universe that we can get away from God, for God is, as the philosopher Plotinus wrote, "*the* Everywhere from which all else takes its existence."[3] Or, as it says in the Acts of the Apostles (17:28), "In him we live and move and have our being." God is present not only in our moments of contemplation, but also in our activities, thus giving us responsibility as co-creators with God.

QUESTIONS FOR REFLECTION AND DISCUSSION

1. Why should Christians not be afraid of the theory of evolution?
2. In what sense or to what degree do you think that evolution might be understood in terms of intelligent design?
3. How are the concepts of God as Sustainer and of God as omnipresent connected? What implications does this connection have for Christian life?

Part II

God as Redeemer

ORDER O...

I OF FAITH

ly, the profession of ...
lebrations. ...

We believe in one G...
the Father, the Almigh...
maker of heaven and earth,
of all that is seen and unseen.

We believe in one Lord, Jesus Chri...
the only Son of God,
eternally begotten of the Fa...
God from God, Light ...
true God from tru...
begotten, not ma...
Through him ...
For us m...
he car...

...ll bow d...
y t...
h...

4

GOD'S ONLY SON

I believe…in Jesus Christ, his only Son, our Lord.
(Apostles' Creed)

We believe in one Lord, Jesus Christ.
(Nicene Creed)

With the creeds' proclamation that we believe in Jesus Christ, we enter the realm of human history. Christianity is based, not on some vague spirituality or philosophical theory, but on a historical claim, a claim on which the legitimacy of Christianity either stands or falls. Yet here we must be careful. History, as a recollection and interpretation of happenings or facts, always involves a *context*—that is, it involves a perspective determined by the observers' location in time and space. This is quite evident in the two creeds we are examining.

Before the baptismal creeds were formed, there were even shorter professions of faith. Simply the name Jesus Christ says a great deal in itself. The title Christ is from a Greek translation (*Christos*) of the Hebrew term *meshiach*, or, as we usually pronounce it, messiah. It literally means "the anointed one"—that is, someone designated as king or high priest. In terms of Old Testament prophecy, it meant the person that was to be sent by God to fulfill God's promises to his people. So in recognizing Jesus as being the Christ, his followers were proclaiming that he was the promised Messiah, so much so that Christ became the equivalent of a surname for

prophet, king, priest

Jesus, and the followers of Jesus soon after became known as Christians.

A much bigger step, however, is taken when we use the word *Lord* as well, even simply saying, "Jesus is Lord!" (see Rom 10:9). Even before the time of Jesus, this title in its Hebrew form, *Adonai*, had become a substitute for *Yahweh*, the most hallowed name of God. In fact, when the Hebrew Scriptures were first translated into Greek, about a century before the time of Jesus, the translators generally used the Greek word *Kyrios* to replace that most sacred name revealed to Moses. So when St. Paul calls Jesus *Kyrios*, or Lord, he seems to be making him almost the equivalent of God. (I say "almost," because St. Paul generally saves the term *ho Theos* or "the God" for the Father alone. Nevertheless, it is clear that, in calling Jesus God's Son, St. Paul is certainly proclaiming Christ's divinity.)

Building on these earliest professions of faith, then, it is evident that the phrase in the Apostles' Creed is saying much the same, except with the addition of the word *only*—"his only Son, our Lord." Why this addition?

At the time when Jesus lived, there were many meanings for the term *Son of God*, and many claims made to that title. For one, the Jews, as God's chosen people, considered them-selves to be God's sons and daughters or collectively "God's son," as we see illustrated by the famous quote from the prophet Hosea in 11:1: "Out of Egypt I have called my Son." (The quote is subsequently used in Matthew 2:15, referring to the Holy Family—and thus Jesus, God's Son—being called back from their flight to Egypt.) We also find the Roman emperors from the time of Caesar Augustus being proclaimed or even proclaiming themselves as divine. So it is quite obvi-ous that the addition of *only* to the earliest proclamations of faith was, first of all, a statement about what scholars call the historical Jesus; that is, the *man*, the *human* Jesus of Nazareth. It is a statement that Jesus alone—no one else, no matter how

holy or favored by God, even Caesar or emperor of the whole
world—is, properly speaking, God's Son.

However, by the time the Council of Nicaea was held, 325
the situation had changed considerably. After a long succession of emperors, some fairly decent, some quite nasty; and of
wars between generals trying to become emperor; and of
others splitting up the job with either colleagues or rivals—no
one, even among the pagans, was apt to take seriously any
emperor's claim to be divine. Still, as Christianity spread
among the Gentile or non-Jewish world, the old temptation to
idolatry was still there, perhaps even intensified in some
ways. Take, for example, Hadrian, one of the more tolerant of
the Roman emperors. Hadrian decided that he might be able
to keep the peace and win more support from the growing
Christian population by placing a statue of Jesus among the
statues in the Pantheon, the famous temple built in Rome in
honor of all the different gods. Of course, the Christians
weren't fooled by this ploy, even if the emperor's intentions
were good. Instead, they continued to recognize only *one* Lord
and God, even if it cost them their lives to remain faithful to
this claim.

Today, however, while we may be tempted to worship
other false gods in the form of money, success, or worldly
power in all its forms, the real challenge to belief in Jesus
Christ as God's only Son comes from quite another source: not
from worldliness, but from our new expanded knowledge of
the world or universe itself. Consider what we now know of
the vastness of the universe, and of not just the possibility but
even the probability of life having evolved on other planets. If
life has evolved elsewhere, how can we be so presumptuous
as to suppose that God would reveal himself exclusively
through the person of Jesus Christ—in other words, that Jesus
alone is God's only begotten Son?

This is not a new question. One of Christianity's earliest
theologians, Origen of Alexandria, thought that life might also
exist elsewhere among the stars. But Origen had so many

ideas out of kilter with ordinary Christian understanding that *this* one wasn't taken very seriously. In the fourteenth century another theologian, the Franciscan friar William of Vaurouillon, began to wonder about this too, and especially about whether or not such intelligent creatures on other planets would also have fallen into, or been affected by, an original sin. If so, would not Christ have to redeem them as well? William's questions were considered to be idle speculation, perhaps something that only Franciscans, following their founder's love of nature, thought about. With Copernicus, the issue was becoming less idle speculation and more of a concern. Two Dominican theologians, Giordano Bruno and Thomas of Campanella, began to address the same questions. In fact, Bruno went so far in some of his questioning, especially regarding the doctrine of the Holy Trinity, that the Inquisition ended up burning him at the stake. After that, it is clear why Galileo's ideas were seen as a threat.

Nevertheless, all this, which may have seemed even to us to be only idle speculation up to a few years ago, now takes on a new relevance, even urgency, in light of our recently expanded knowledge of the universe. And as we shall soon see, what the Council of Nicaea was to add to the ancient baptismal creeds, although the bishops may have been entirely unaware of its consequences at the time, would eventually challenge the Christian understanding of God, and of God's workings in the universe, to enter a whole new level—one that we are still trying to fully comprehend today.

QUESTIONS FOR REFLECTION AND DISCUSSION

1.   In what way is history especially important for Christianity?
2.   Why was it so important for the early Christians to insist on Jesus being God's *only* Son?

3. What is the significance of the title Lord as applied to Jesus, and what does this title imply for Christian life today?

4. Do you think God may have revealed himself in the way he did in Jesus elsewhere in the universe? Why or why not?

Oswald Chambers –
Give up right to yourself.
Surrender –
How this compares to Islam

5

TRUE GOD FROM TRUE GOD

... the only Son of God, eternally begotten of the Father,
God from God, Light from Light, true God from true God...
(Nicene Creed)

The historical setting changed gradually during the first three centuries of Christianity, but in the early days of the fourth century, a major and sudden upheaval took place. In the year 312, one of the rivals for the imperial throne was a general named Constantine. He claimed that he had received a heavenly vision promising that he would conquer in the name of Christ, and almost immediately he won a crucial battle outside Rome, defeating his rival Maxentius and becoming the new ruler of the Roman Empire.

The following year Constantine issued his famous Edict of Milan. Sometimes called the Edict of Toleration, it not only officially proclaimed toleration for Christianity within the empire, it also paved the way for Christianity to eventually become the official religion of the Roman Empire. His mother, now known as St. Helena, journeyed to Jerusalem to try to find the relic of the true cross. Meanwhile Constantine began a massive program of church building, beginning in Rome and extending throughout the whole empire. He also became passionately convinced that it was his duty to unite all Christians in a way that could leave no doubt as to what they believed, especially regarding the identity of Jesus Christ himself. Constantine's primary reason for doing so, however,

compare constantine 34 purpose + method - unite
with God's purpose + method - unity

seems to have been political: he simply thought that he could not afford to have an empire that was deeply divided on religious lines.

Until this time, while all Christians could agree that Jesus is the Son of God and Lord, there was a wide divergence as to what this really meant. All seemed to agree that Jesus was divine—that he was sent by or had his origin in God and shared many of God's qualities. But how to explain this and still maintain the unity of God?

Many, perhaps even most, thought of Jesus as *man*; that is, an ordinary human being who was specially graced or endowed by the Holy Spirit and who, as a result of this special gift of the Spirit, could then be called in a very special way the Son of God. The only argument among these people, who based their point of view mostly on the first three Gospels, was exactly when this special transformation of the human nature of Jesus actually happened. Some, following Mark's Gospel, said it took place when Jesus was baptized in the Jordan River by John the Baptist. Others pointed to the infancy stories found at the beginning of the Gospels of Matthew and Luke and said it happened at the very moment that Jesus was conceived. Still others, looking to the Acts of the Apostles and some of the early writings of the apostle Paul, even thought it might have not been completely true until Jesus was raised from the dead!

There was another school of thought, based mostly on a literal reading of the Gospel attributed to John, the beloved disciple. In the beginning of that Gospel, we are told that the Word, who was God, became flesh. Understood literally, this seemed to be saying that Jesus was God taking on a human body—but *only* a human body, not a human mind or soul. In other words, Jesus was God walking around in a kind of human suit, something like the way we walk around in a new suit of clothes! Obviously, something had to be done to settle this disagreement.

Not that no one had ever tried. Certain Christians, especially those who were converts from Judaism, tended to think of Jesus as neither man, nor God, but something in between, perhaps an angel sent by God. Others thought of Jesus simply as an apparition of God pretending to be human. But at this point in history, a priest in Alexandria, Egypt, by the name of Arius, decided that, with the help of the Greek philosophy of Platonism, he could solve the problem. Christ, according to Arius and his followers (and he had many), was a quasi-divine being, but not really or truly God. While many bishops were convinced that Arius held the key to understanding who or what Jesus really was, many others, especially in the eastern part of the empire, were already greatly disturbed by Arius's ideas.

At this point, Constantine had already moved the administrative capital of the empire far to the east to a Greek city then called Byzantium, which he renamed Constantinople after himself (modern-day Istanbul). He did this primarily to keep better control of political developments, but he also saw a potential threat to the unity of the empire over this doctrinal dispute. So in 325 Constantine summoned all the bishops he could to one of his new palaces in the nearby town of Nicaea. It is estimated that there were about 1,800 bishops in the world at the time, but only about 300 or so—tradition says there were 318—showed up, almost all of them from the Eastern Mediterranean world. Nevertheless, Bishop Hosius of Cordova, Spain, who was Constantine's advisor in matters of religion, presided, with two priests from Rome representing Pope Sylvester, while Emperor Constantine himself personally mediated between the various bishops and constantly pled with them to find a solution that might be agreeable to all.

The result was that major additions were made to the earlier creed. A number of these additions—especially the phrases *eternally begotten*, *Light from Light*, and *true God from true God*—had been suggested previously by a regional council or synod of bishops that had met several times at Antioch in Syria to counter the growing influence of Arius and his followers. By saying that "the only Son" was "eternally begotten of the Father," these bishops intended to counter Arius's claim that the Son, as "the firstborn of all creation" (Col 1:15), obviously had been born, if not in time, at least at the beginning of time. In fact, both the Greek and Latin text of the Nicene Creed at one time had "before the ages" after "begotten" (as well as "from the substance of the Father") to emphasize this point. So in adopting this language from these earlier meetings, the bishops at Nicaea were affirming their belief in Christ being fully or truly divine. Then, by adding "Light from Light"—Jesus, "the light of the world" (John 8:12; 9:5), coming from God, "the Father of lights" (Jas 1:17)—the bishops stated even more clearly that Christ is "true God from true God."

So far so good, at least in literary or scriptural terms. But as we shall soon see, it still seemed to many of the bishops that even this language perhaps wasn't quite clear enough. And yet today, as we look at this attempt to step behind the data regarding the historical Jesus, back into the realm of the eternal nature of God before all time, we may be struck by its brashness or audacity.

Do we really believe that the Holy Spirit guides the Church, or perhaps even inspires individuals or small groups (such as the bishops gathered at Nicaea) with new insights? If so, then we may have to conclude that in some way these bishops, nearly seventeen centuries ago, were not only addressing the needs of their time, but also anticipating the challenges of our own age. For what they were telling us is not just that God chose to step down, as it were, out of his eternity to share a creature-like existence with us at one point and one place in time. Certainly it was that—but perhaps it was also much more. The incarnation of God, in a very special way, was a sign or demonstration of God's giving of God's own self for the salvation or redemption or even—as St. Thomas Aquinas tells us—the "completion" of all creation. The only difference between then, when the bishops at Nicaea formulated this doctrine, and now, as we try to probe its meaning, is that we are much more aware of what a cosmic and ongoing or continuing process this now must be seen to be.

QUESTIONS FOR REFLECTION AND DISCUSSION

1. In the context of subsequent history, do you see Constantine's intervention to have been providential or not?
2. Do you regard the additions made at Nicaea as having clarified matters or not? Did they make it easier or harder for you to believe?
3. What challenge does Nicaea present for the future of belief?

Christianity began in Palestine as
an experience.

It moved to Greece + became
a philosophy

It shifted to Italy and became
an institution

It arrived in Europe and became
a culture

It travelled to America and
became a business.

-6-

ONE IN BEING

...true God from true God, begotten, not made,
one in Being with the Father. Through him all things were made.
of one Being
(Nicene Creed)

vs Alexandria

The bishops at Nicaea added three more significant changes
to the cluster of phrases borrowed from the Antioch synod.
They began these additions with a repetition of *God from God*,
but with the addition of *true* before both mentions of God.
This was significant in itself, because it eliminates any possibility of considering Jesus Christ as a "lesser" God—someone
Arius
less divine than God the Father. Likewise, we see the repetition of the term *begotten*, this time with the addition of *not
made*, emphasizing the Son's divinity and ruling out any idea
of him being a creature, no matter how much he is exalted. All
this makes it very clear that this section of the Nicene Creed is
speaking of the eternal generation of the Son, not yet about his
birth in time.

Almost as if all this were not clear enough, the doctrine
next adds a word that has been translated in the 1973 American
Catholic version of the Nicene Creed as "one in being," where
most of the English-speaking world, echoing the Latin translation, uses "consubstantial." From the very beginning, this addition to the older baptismal creed has proved to be most
contentious. In Greek, the adjective *homoousios* meant "[of] the
same stuff" or "same substance." Arius had used this word, but
rejected applying it to Christ when he first denied that Christ

was equal to the Father or Almighty God. So the bishops decided that they had no choice but to use Arius's own terminology to counter his claims. Even then, other bishops suggested a one-letter addition, the famous "one iota" (the Greek name for the letter i), changing the term to *homoiousios*—which would soften the meaning to "similar to" rather than "the same." Still, many of the bishops were apparently unhappy with the use of the word *ousia* to begin with. It made it sound as if God were a material substance that could be cut into pieces or divided up. Nevertheless, despite mental reservations, the majority went along with the wording, as non-biblical as it was, thus leaving *us* with the still-unfinished task of how this strange word should be translated.

There followed yet another assertion of Christ's divinity, but this time in much more biblical language: "Through him all things were made." This statement is almost a word-for-word quotation from the prologue of John's Gospel, and not even Arius could disagree with it. This was also followed at Nicaea by the addition of "things in heaven and things on earth." (It was later dropped at Constantinople.)

Nevertheless, the result was not what Constantine had hoped. Many of the bishops who had been present, even those who agreed with Constantine's intentions of a unity of doctrine, had strong reservations about what they had signed. In the Eastern part of the Church, in particular, many of the bishops remained semi-Arian, meaning that although they believed Jesus is truly divine, they still regarded him in some ways as subordinate to, or less than, God the Father. So the doctrine articulated at Nicaea was not universally accepted, or was accepted only with some hesitation, until the doctrine was further confirmed at the First Council of Constantinople in 381. Even after that, some bishops, such as Nestorius, the archbishop-patriarch of Constantinople, accepted this teaching only by making a strong distinction between the eternal Word or Son of God and the human Jesus, in whom, through the power of God's Spirit, they believed this Word dwelt. As a result, they went so far as to deny to Mary the by-then pop-ular title *theotokos*, which, translated literally, means "the one who gives birth to God," but which—at least in that ancient understanding of reproductive biology discussed earlier—was taken to be the equivalent of calling her "mother of God." So in 431 a council held at Ephesus condemned anyone who ever used such an evasion to deny that "she brought forth after the flesh [i.e., in a physical manner] the Word of God who became flesh."

Unfortunately, the reaction against Nestorius paved the way for a more subtle form of the old heresy of Docetism, which taught that Christ was not really human but only appeared to be human. This time the heresy was promoted by another churchman in Constantinople named Eutyches, whose teaching became known as *monophysitism*—meaning that Christ possessed a *single* nature (*physis*) that was under-stood as an amalgam: part human, part divine.

In the face of this continuing controversy, still another council had to be called to resolve the issue. The Council of Chalcedon, held in 451 under the watchful eyes of the emperor Marcion and the empress Pulcheria, reaffirmed the teachings of both Nicaea and Ephesus that Jesus was and is truly God; it also proclaimed that Jesus was truly and fully a *human* being—that he is "consubstantial" or *homoousios* with *us*, as well as with God. It also asserted that although both his human and divine *natures* are distinct and complete, in him they cannot be separated and thus they form a single *person* who is both God and man. In other words, while we may refer to Jesus as a human being, we may also speak of him as God.

The difficulty of reconciling these two statements has never been completely resolved. Many scholars, especially some New Testament specialists, advocate that we go back to the first three Gospels and see Jesus as basically a human being given a special task by God. These scholars consider the evangelist John's close identification of Christ with Almighty God as somewhat exaggerated theological embellishment.

Such a view, however, clearly contradicts what was taught by the councils of Nicaea, Ephesus, and Chalcedon—the great "Christological Councils." It also comes close to denying that the author of the Fourth Gospel was divinely inspired to see more deeply into the mystery of the eternal origin of Jesus Christ.

On the other hand, a few scholars have suggested that Jesus really is God's Word in human form, but that the difficulty consists in imagining that Word as actually a second *person* in God from all eternity. They say that perhaps, like divine Wisdom was personified in the Hebrew Scriptures, so too, was the divine Word—until it actually did become a real person in Jesus Christ. Such a view, however, would seem to require a radical reinterpretation of what we mean by God as a trinity. And it would also raise another problem, for if the Word of God is not in some sense an actual person in its own right before its incarnation in Jesus, how could that same Word ever be incarnated at other times or even at the same time elsewhere in the universe? While this question may seem far-fetched, no doubt it must have occurred to those theologians and other churchmen who may have been present at the special conference convened at the Vatican in November 2009, where astronomers and biologists were invited to speak about the possibilities and likelihood of the existence of life, even intelligent life, elsewhere in the universe.

No less a scholar than Karl Rahner, who was perhaps the Catholic Church's greatest theologian in the twentieth century, has thoughtfully engaged this question. Rahner once suggested that the term *person* had so changed its meaning between the time of these great councils and our own time that it might be prudent to call a moratorium on the use of this word when it comes to God, especially when it comes to our attempts to explain the Trinity. While such a policy would undoubtedly necessitate some reformulation of our cate-chisms, it would be more in line with the Council of Nicaea, which avoided pronouncing on such matters, and with the

Council of Chalcedon, which applied the use of the word *person* (*prosopon* in Greek) to what theologians call the hypostatic union—the union of the divine and human natures, but not two different or separate persons, in Jesus.

QUESTIONS FOR REFLECTION AND DISCUSSION

1. Which translation of *homoousios*—"consubstantial" or "one in being"—makes more sense to you? Why?

2. Do you think that the Council of Chalcedon, by insisting that Christ is also *homoousios* with us in his humanity, succeeded in clarifying matters?

3. Do you know any Christians who, without realizing it, still hold either Nestorian or monophysite views today? If so, do you think the Nicene Creed should be revised?

4. What do you think about Rahner's suggestion—that is, having a moratorium on using the word *person* in terms of the Trinity?

Person — In Western culture equated with the individual, isolated, autonomous. (Descartes)
But today—
Personhood constituted by relationships.
We depend on others in order to be ourselves.
Distinct from others but realize ourselves in + through others in communion

7

BORN OF THE VIRGIN MARY

...who was conceived by the Holy Spirit and
born of the virgin Mary...
(Apostles' Creed)

For us men and for our salvation he came down from heaven,
was incarnate of the Holy Spirit and the Virgin Mary...
(Nicene Creed)

When the Apostles' Creed speaks of Jesus as "conceived by the Holy Spirit," the Nicene Creed refers once more to Jesus' eternal or heavenly origins, proclaiming our belief that Jesus "came down from heaven" and, as the new English translation expresses it, became "incarnate of the Virgin Mary" (the long-used translation for Catholics in the United States said, "was born of the virgin Mary and became man"). Either way, at this point we move back into the realm of human history here on earth.

Yet here we must be careful. In the study of history there frequently exists a tension between what actually happened and the stories through which the historical events are told. In 1964 the Vatican's official biblical commission made a careful distinction between what it sees as three different levels or stages of tradition contained within the Gospels: *First*, there is the actual record or memories of what Jesus did and said. *Second*, there is the basic truth or message (the *kerygma*) of salvation as preached by the apostles. And *third*, there are the various approaches, themes, or theological interpretations used by the various gospel authors to convey their basic message. This third level is one of the main reasons there are four different Gospels and not just one.

Nevertheless, if Jesus of Nazareth was a historical human being, it is obvious that he had to have been born. But it does not seem that Jesus himself ever gave an account of how that came to be. In fact, John's Gospel (see John 7:28; 8:19; 19:9) tells us that when Jesus was challenged to account for his earthly origins, he refused to give any definite answer. Even the scriptures themselves do not totally agree on this point. The earliest written testimony, that of the apostle Paul, simply says that he was "born of a woman" (Gal 4:4) and that he was "descended from David according to the flesh" (Rom 1:3). The earliest Gospel, that of Mark, begins with the baptism of Jesus in the Jordan and says nothing much about his origins other than that his mother and his brothers were worried about his sanity. Only the Gospels of Matthew and Luke contain infancy narratives that tell the story of a virginal conception and a birth in Bethlehem, but even here they differ on some major details. Matthew has the Holy Family fleeing into Egypt from Herod's wrath. But Luke, who claims at the beginning of his Gospel that he carefully inquired into all these matters, instead has them peacefully visiting the Temple in Jerusalem and then returning directly to their hometown, Nazareth, in Galilee.

When we compare these two infancy stories, the only thing we can arrive at with reasonable certainty is that, while they both have their origins in a common tradition that Jesus was born in Bethlehem, the only certain historical knowledge we have of his earthly origins is that his birth occurred around 4 BCE (that is, Before the Common, or Current, Era), and that his mother, Mary, was a young virgin, espoused to a humble workman named Joseph from a small town, called Nazareth in Galilee.

As for the Fourth Gospel, John seems only to hint at the stories of Jesus' miraculous origins but does not attempt to include any details about Jesus' early life on earth. Instead, John emphasized the preexistence of the Son by using the same Greek philosophical concept that the Jewish philosopher Philo of Alexandria did when describing God's Wisdom as it is portrayed in some of the later books of the Old Testament. This *Logos*, usually translated as "Word" or sometimes as "reason," was seen as the knowing or directing divine intelligence that is present throughout the universe.

When we compare the infancy narratives in Matthew and Luke, each with its different emphasis and development of a common tradition, and contrast them to the very different approach used in the Fourth Gospel, we must conclude that they all belong to that third stage of the tradition as outlined by the Vatican's biblical commission. Yet, however they may differ from one another, it is obvious that each of them was written to illustrate the central, indeed the most distinctive, belief of Christianity, which is that God was present in Jesus in a unique and mysterious way. To repeat: these different methods were each designed with one object in mind, and that was to point to a single major truth, which is simply that *for our sake, God has entered into human history in the person of Jesus Christ*. And it is this last point in particular that is emphasized by the Nicene Creed. Borrowing directly from the language of John's Gospel, this creed uses the graphic term *sarkothena* (in Latin, *incarnatus est*; either way, literally "to become flesh") to emphasize the startling claim that God actually became a man, with all that it involves.

Why this repeated emphasis on the flesh-and-blood reality of Jesus Christ? Most immediately, in the context of the Nicene Creed, it may have been added as a balance to the *homoousios* statement of the preceding section. But most importantly, it constituted yet another defense of authentic Christian belief against the earliest heresy, that of Docetism (from the Greek, *dokein* = "to appear"), which asserted that Jesus Christ was not really human but only appeared to be human. We even see this heresy being attacked in the First and Second Letters of John in the New Testament, which denounce as "a deceiver" and "the antichrist" those who deny "that Jesus Christ has come in the flesh" (1 John 4:2 and 2 John 7). Yet the tendency to deny Christ's humanity remained strong, especially among the Gnostics, who preferred to think of Jesus as a heavenly spirit only pretending to be a human being, something like an actor pretending to be someone else by wearing a special mask. So widespread was this tendency that in the fourth century, St. Gregory of Nazianzus, one of the Church's greatest preachers and theologians, used a phrase that has long served as an axiom to test any teaching regarding the incarnation. It is simply this: "What wasn't assumed has not been redeemed!"

Again, why is the flesh-and-blood reality of the incarnation so important to Christian belief? Why couldn't God simply redeem us, as it were, "from on high," out of his divine generosity? After all, did not God forgive his own chosen people after they failed him, again and again?

Down through Christian history many attempts have been made to answer this question. In general, the answers fall under one of two categories. First there is the atonement theory, put forward in its best known formulation by St. Anselm of Canterbury in the eleventh century. In his treatise *Cur Deus homo* ("Why God Became Man"), Anselm argued that because God, who is infinite, had been offended, only God would be capable of making up for the infinite damage that was done. Yet, since it was humans who had committed the offense, then the person who made up for it had to be, at the same time, a human who would be fully representative of the whole human race. The emphasis here is on atonement for sin.

The other theory is less centered on sin and guilt and is much more cosmic or universal in its scope. First advanced in the second century by St. Irenaeus, who apparently took his theme from St. Paul's description of all creation being subject to "futility" (Rom 8:20), it sees redemption as a new, second creation, where Jesus plays the part of a new Adam, reversing the effects of Adam's sin on all creation. This theology of reca-pitulation, as St. Irenaeus termed it, sees Christ's redemptive activity as reaching out to all aspects and levels of creation, drawing it after him as the new head of the human race. It was expanded further by Origen of Alexandria to include the redemption of *all* creatures. (Origen perhaps went too far, including redemption of even the devil himself!) No less a theologian than the great St. Thomas Aquinas said before his death that, among the reasons for which God became man, "The Incarnation puts the finishing touch to the whole vast work envisaged by God."[4] *unity — Love*

QUESTIONS FOR REFLECTION AND DISCUSSION

1. Which of the two translations of this passage of the Nicene Creed—"became incarnate of the Virgin Mary" or "was born of the virgin Mary and became man"—makes more sense to you?

2. Which of the gospel accounts of Christ's origins do you find most convincing, and why?

3. Evaluate the importance of the incarnation for Christian faith.

4. The thirteenth-century Franciscan theologian John Duns Scotus, who went even further than Aquinas, believed that the incarnation might have occurred even without original sin having taken place. What do you think?

*Original Sin —
emergence of self-consciousness
(∴ choice, otherness) in evolution*

8

CRUCIFIED AND DIED

He suffered under Pontius Pilate, was crucified, died,
and was buried. He descended into hell.
(Apostles' Creed)

For our sake he was crucified under Pontius Pilate;
he suffered, died, and was buried.
(Nicene Creed)

If the actual origins of Jesus remain shrouded in mystery and apparent contradiction even within the sacred scriptures, just the opposite is true when it comes to his death. Nothing is more historically verifiable about Jesus than that he was crucified, died, and was buried—yet curiously, the Nicene Creed, at least in the Greek and Latin texts, doesn't explicitly mention the word *death*, only that he suffered, apparently taking it for granted that it was even unto death. Nevertheless, the Roman historian Tacitus (AD 56–118) in his *Annals,* and the Jewish historian Flavius Josephus (AD 37–101), who wrote his *Antiquities* around the year 94, reported this event. Both mention that Jesus had been put to death by Pilate, during the reign of the emperor Tiberius, and although neither gives the exact date, historians have concluded that it took place at Passover time around AD 28 to 30. As a routine Roman-style execution carried out by a governor notorious for the number of crucifixions he had commanded during his career, we could hardly expect any more detailed records than we already have. What should interest us most is why Jesus died and what it means for us.

We have already been given a theological reason in the Nicene Creed. Just as the incarnation was "for us and for our salvation," so also Jesus' crucifixion and death was "for our sake." Of course, Pilate didn't see it that way. He was merely executing what he saw as a source of trouble, a potential case of a riot at the most volatile time of year in Jerusalem, when crowds of pilgrims arrived there for the High Holy Days surrounding the feast of Passover. Whether Jesus was actually guilty or not of inciting a riot really didn't concern him. Pilate saw it as his primary job, under the circumstances, not to administer justice but to do whatever he must in order to keep the peace.

It is very important that Christians understand this. Christians have shed too much Jewish blood down through the ages to ignore the importance of a truly historical understanding of this event. Not that a theological understanding isn't also important—but an accurate theological understanding is almost impossible without first setting the historical record straight. The Jewish people, as a whole, were not guilty of the death of Jesus. At the very most, certain of their leaders (the higher ranks of the Temple priesthood, most of whom belonged to the Sadducee party that collaborated with the Romans) delivered Jesus up to Pilate. They feared that the actions and teachings of Jesus would cause what little remaining power they had over their people to be taken away by the Roman authorities. In part, they were right. The reform of the Jewish religion that Jesus seemed to embody very well might have had serious political as well as religious side effects. Jesus was truly a religious revolutionary. What he stood for was something very different from the formalized temple ceremonial practiced by the Jewish high priests in Jerusalem and their idea that God was to be worshiped and sin wiped out by the offering of incense and other gifts, and especially by the ritualized shedding of blood.

Another reason it is so important that we understand, is that we don't automatically equate sacrifice with something involving bloodshed. The word *sacrifice* simply or literally means to "make (something) holy" or to "consecrate," or to set aside something as dedicated to God or destined for a holy purpose. Indeed, some of the "sacrifices" described in the Old Testament (such as the "show bread" placed in the sanctuary) were of this nature. Not every sacrifice need be a holocaust. Indeed, even the New Testament (Hebrews 10:5–7) pictures the essence of Christ's sacrifice not as a sacrificial holocaust, but as carrying out God's will as described in Psalm 40.

Nevertheless, almost from the beginning of Christianity, there has been an emphasis on the death of Christ as a sacrifice that in some way parallels the bloody sacrifices described in the Old Testament. The theme is obvious in John's Gospel where Jesus is called the Lamb of God and his death is pictured as having taken place not on Passover itself but on the Day of Preparation, when the paschal lambs were slaughtered. It is also obvious in the apostle Paul's writings, and especially in the Epistle to the Hebrews where the author describes Christ as the new high priest who is, at the same time, the sacrificial victim. No doubt this comparison came quite naturally to the first Christians, especially the early Jewish Christians, who had experienced the trauma of the bloody death of Jesus and were also familiar with the old ritualized sacrifices to God. Yet we must be very careful as to how we apply these comparisons.

At this point it has to be said very clearly that Jesus died, not as a victim offered to appease an angry God, or even as a scapegoat for our own sinfulness, as comforting for some people as these images may be. It is not God who has to be appeased or persuaded to forgive us. God has already forgiven us. It is not God but our own human nature that compels us to make amends by offering sacrifice. So it must be made clear that what Jesus was really doing, in his role as both priest and victim, was to give expression to God's

Ps. – capacity to hear & obey (Thy will be done)
your will is within my heart (Heb 10:5–9)

redeeming love by giving himself over, in the most graphic way possible, in a complete act of loving self-surrender, and that he did so in our place and in a way that forever reconciles the human race with God.

Did Jesus really want it to happen exactly in this way? If the story of his agony in the Garden of Gethsemane is any indication, it was not his first choice. But he also knew that if we were to be convinced of what a total love of God means, then, under the circumstances, there was no other way out. The recently rediscovered *Gospel of Judas* is quite obviously an attempt by early Christian Gnostics to reinterpret Christianity to their own liking. Yet if it has any historical worth at all, it only reinforces what is clear in the four canonical Gospels—that Jesus knew he must die to accomplish God's purposes and even, to some extent, cooperated with the traitor who was in their midst.

Yet why did accomplishing God's purposes have to lead even to his own death? The biblical love poetry in the Song of Songs says, "Love is [as] strong as death" (Song 8:6). It would seem that Jesus' own commentary on that verse is "No one has greater love than this, to lay down one's life for one's friends" (John 15:13). Only in the act of his own dying could Jesus fully demonstrate God's love for us. And so he really did die "for us and our salvation," but not because God would otherwise be angry with us, but because God loves us so much.

The Apostles' Creed adds to all this one more detail: not only was he buried (as the Nicene Creed also says), but he also "descended into hell." Most Christians find this ancient statement very puzzling. In fact it is a very old scriptural theme. Still, some Latin versions of the Apostles' Creed have *inferos* (meaning "that which is below") instead of *inferna* (which means a "furnace"), while a more recent version of the Apostles' Creed used in the United States simply substitutes the word *death* in place of the word *hell*. In contrast, the Greek form of this ancient baptismal creed, like the Nicene Creed, omits this sentence altogether. But what this ancient tradition had in mind was the idea, found in 1 Peter 3:19 among a few other places, that in the act of dying Jesus was entering, not into hell as a place of punishment, but rather the "abode of the dead" (*sheol*, or "the pit," in Hebrew; *hades*, or "the underworld," in Greek). So the substitution of *inferos* in Latin in place of *inferna* seems to have been the result of attempting to correct the mistaken notion that the soul or spirit of Jesus was undergoing punishment.

In any case, the point is this: because of his human nature, Jesus had to undergo death, just like the rest of us. This was an integral part of the demonstration of God's love for us in the life of his Son—that everything we must face in our living, he too went through. And he will be with each of us as we go through our own death as well. Jesus, as the Epistle to the Hebrews tells us, is the "forerunner on our behalf" and "pioneer in [our] faith." (See Heb 6:20 and 12:1b–2: the word for "our" does not appear in the Greek original of the latter text; however, most translations assume this to be understood.) Either way, if we follow him, even in our own dying, we will find that our own faith is perfected and brought to completion in union with Christ.

QUESTIONS FOR REFLECTION AND DISCUSSION

1. Why do you think that the Jewish people as a whole have been so often blamed for the death of Jesus?
2. Does the theme of Jesus' death as a bloody sacrifice for our sins make much sense to you? Why or why not?
3. Does the ancient theme of Christ's "descent into hell" speak to you in any way?
4. Explain how Jesus, in undergoing his death, can serve as a model for our faith.

9

RISEN FROM THE DEAD

On the third day he rose again from the dead.
(Apostles' Creed)

On the third day he rose again according to the Scriptures.
(Nicene Creed)

At this point the two creeds are all but identical. Except for the Apostles' Creed's addition of "from the dead"—which by now should be obvious—both creeds are repeating a formula passed down from the earliest apostolic message (*kerygma*) or preaching. The only significant variation is that, while the earliest renditions of this formula tend to speak of Jesus being "raised," the creedal version, much like in Luke's Gospel and occasionally in Matthew, stresses the idea that the resurrection was within Christ's own powers.

Either way, the assertion that Jesus—in whose person the Word or Son of God became incarnate and who was crucified, died, and was buried under Pontius Pilate—has been raised or rose from the dead and still now lives is Christianity's boldest and most contested claim. Still, both creeds continue to repeat this claim by means of this formula, apparently passed down from the apostles: "On the third day he rose again according to the Scriptures." This in turn reflects the older belief—evidenced in the life and belief of Jesus himself—that, even according to *his* interpretation of the Old Testament, the Messiah, or Christ, after being killed, would rise again.

54

No where in Jewish [?] it was it assumed that the messiah would die die.

From the very beginning, however, there were counter-claims. According to Matthew's account (28:11–15), certain Jews bribed the guards at the tomb to claim that the body of Jesus had been stolen while they were asleep—a rather lame excuse, for as one of the early commentators pointed out, if the soldiers were asleep, how would they know? Others would claim that Jesus didn't really die or even, as did Mohammed and his followers centuries later, that someone else died on the cross in his place, while Jesus ascended directly to heaven, never to be seen again until the final Judgment Day.

There is, of course, great skepticism over any concept of *resurrection* to begin with. The conservative Jewish Sadducees in Judea denied the possibility. And as St. Paul found out to his consternation during his address to the more educated people in Athens, the Greek word *anastasia* (which means "to rise again") made it sound as if Paul was talking about a goddess. It was the shock of this incomprehension that seems to have caused Paul to rethink his understanding of what a resurrection of the body might be. Surely it is something more than the resuscitation of a corpse. As a result, Paul seems to have revised his formulation, stressing the spiritual nature of the risen body and contrasting it to the mortal, corruptible body buried in death (see especially 1 Cor 15:44).

Still, we must ask, what real evidence do we have to ground this belief of ours? Admittedly, the various gospel accounts of who experienced the risen Jesus seemingly conflict with one another: scripture scholars who have tried for centuries to harmonize these accounts seem to have worked in vain—which in turn leads to the observation that if all these stories had been simply made up, a very poor job of it had been done.

Nevertheless, what we have, *to begin with, is a collection of stories about an empty tomb* originating from the small group of women who had followed Jesus from Galilee and had stood by him at the cross to the very end. At first no one believed their claims that they had seen an angel announcing that Jesus had risen—not until, according to John's account, he and Peter inspected the empty tomb. Only then did they begin to believe.

Next, we have reports of various *encounters with a living physical person* who was not immediately recognizable, but who revealed his identity by various stages and in different manners to those who were open to belief. These encounters with the resurrected Jesus himself included those experienced by Mary Magdalene, by the two disciples on the road to Emmaus (one of whom we are told was named Cleophas), and by ten of the chosen apostles gathered in the upper room (later eleven, when Thomas finally showed up). We might call these concrete, or physical, encounters with the risen Christ.

In addition to the above is the encounter experienced by some five hundred others at the same time, mentioned by Paul in 1 Corinthians 15:6. The five hundred must have included Mary, the mother of Jesus, and other women who were loyal followers of Jesus. At least some of them, according to St. Paul, were still alive at the time (around the year 57) when he was writing his First Letter to the Corinthians. The veracity of these witnesses is further evidence, testified to by *their willingness to give their whole lives* to the cause of spreading the good news, as indeed many of them did, including Paul himself, to the point of shedding their own blood.

There is final evidence of the resurrection that has to be considered: *the lives (and deaths) of those "who have not seen, yet still believe"* (John 20:29). Christianity grew, even if slowly at first, during the lifetime of the apostles, then more spectacularly in the ancient world after their deaths, primarily because of the example of their followers. "See how these Christians love one another!" wrote one observer at the time. Nor did they love just "one another"; in fact, the pagan world wondered in amazement at the example given by the Christian community in Alexandria, Egypt, when that city was swept by a devastating plague toward the middle of the third century. Instead of fleeing to the countryside as most common-sense people would do, many Christians stayed behind to minister to the sick, both Christian and pagan alike, often at the cost of their own lives. In succeeding ages, monasteries often became known for their infirmaries, beginning a long tradition of Christian-run hospitals, clinics, and medical missions around the world, led by people like Fr. Damian (the leper-saint of Molokai); Mother (now declared Blessed) Teresa of Calcutta; and the "Protestant Saint," Dr. Albert Schweitzer, a world-famous theologian and musician who gave up his academic career and the concert hall to serve the poor in Africa. It is people like these who have been and who continue to be the contemporary evidence of the power of the resurrected Christ.

Looking at these various levels of evidence, ranging from the physical appearances of the risen Christ, to their psychological impact on the lives and deaths of those first witnesses in testimony to what they had seen, and finally to the spiritual legacy of all those who have lived their lives according to the example of Christ, I think we can begin to understand the observation of the deeply religious Russian Orthodox philosopher Nikolai Berdyaev, who described the resurrection of Christ as being not merely a historical event that can be located back in time, but a "meta-historical" event that continues beyond the limits of time and space, much as the spiritual or metaphysical world transcends the physical world of matter. This in turn explains why ultimately, even in the case of the Eucharist, the sacramental Body and Blood of Christ, it is "the spirit that gives life" (John 6:63).

All this, however, places a special obligation on us who have been baptized. Much of the time, if you ask Christians what Jesus accomplished by his resurrection, the answer will be that this was the way he proved he really was God. Yet that is not primarily the way the scriptures treat it. Instead, we find over and over again in the New Testament that God raised Jesus from the dead in order to bring us new life. As St. Paul put it in his First Epistle to the Corinthians (15:22): "Just as all die in Adam, so all will be made alive in Christ." Or, again, we find in Colossians 2:12: "You were buried with him in baptism, in which you were also raised with him in faith." In other words, in this most ancient line of Christian theology, just as the death of Jesus is seen as having canceled out the effects of sin (summarized by death, or at least our fear of death), so too the rising of Jesus is seen as being the source of new life. As an ancient Byzantine Easter chant puts it: "Christ is risen from the dead! He has crushed death by his death and bestowed life upon those who lay in the tomb."

If all this is true, then it is easy to see why the proof of Christ's resurrection cannot simply be in what the apostles and others saw on the first Easter and in the days afterward, but must also be in what people see in Christians today. Paul argues: "Therefore we have been buried with him by baptism into death, so that, just as Christ was raised from the dead by the glory of the Father, we too might walk in newness of life" (Rom 6:4). But if this newness of life is the mark of a Christian and a prerequisite for our own resurrection, then it would seem to follow that a failure to live in this newness of life is itself a denial of the resurrection, and that all the miracles and wonders of nearly two thousand years ago are not apt to convince people today unless the effects are visible in our lives.

In other words, what is being said here—over and over again in our scriptures and in our worship each day and especially on each Sunday—is that it was not just Jesus' death on the cross that won us God's forgiveness. Even more, it was Christ's resurrection from the tomb that brings us new life. But, instead of merely celebrating it, we must now live this new life to the full.

QUESTIONS FOR REFLECTION AND DISCUSSION

1. Considering all the various claims, pro and con, regarding the resurrection of Jesus, what would they seem to prove?
2. If the bones of Jesus were actually found, would this necessarily destroy our belief? Why or why not?
3. In what sense can the resurrection of Jesus be seen as *meta-historical* event?
4. What is the sacramental meaning of baptism and what are its implications for Christian living?

10

ASCENDED INTO HEAVEN

He ascended into heaven and is seated at the
right hand of the Father almighty.
(Apostle's Creed)

He ascended into heaven and is seated at the
right hand of the Father.
(Nicene Creed)

If the resurrection takes us beyond history in its usual sense, the ascension of Christ as described in the creeds, which are virtually identical on this point, takes us beyond space and, it seems, beyond time itself.

In the Acts of the Apostles, Luke describes the apostles' vision of Christ ascending from Jerusalem's Mount of Olives forty days after his resurrection. Matthew's Gospel gives less detail, and instead places the final appearance of Jesus before the apostles as taking place in Galilee. The original version of Mark's Gospel leaves us outside the tomb, still wondering, while later versions of Mark have additional verses that appear to be modeled on Luke's account. John, on the other hand, does not even mention the ascension; he seems to think of Jesus, almost immediately after his resurrection, as moving back and forth from his risen state in heaven to manifesting his victory over death here on earth. So once again we are confronted not so much with historical recollections as with different stories designed to convey a religious truth that defies description in any terms of normal human experience.

If that is true about the ascension of Jesus, it is certainly even more so when it comes to the description of him as being "seated at the right hand of the Father." The picture of someone sitting at the right hand of a king or ruler is standard biblical language for a place of honor—not unlike our expression of calling someone a "right-hand man" if that person is particularly valuable. It is figurative or strictly symbolic, even poetic, language.

The important truth about the location of the post-ascension Jesus is that, if heaven means being with God, and since God is everywhere, then, at least in one sense, heaven is everywhere. Yet, since it is a state or condition of existence rather than a place, then we might even say heaven is no place in particular. Certainly it is not above the clouds somewhere or off among the stars or distant galaxies. Instead, let us turn to Ephesians 1:23, in which Paul, speaking of the glorified Christ, tells us that he is the head of the Church, "which is his body, the fullness of him who fills all in all"—or, as *The Jerusalem Bible* translates it, "the whole of creation."

Again, St. Paul is not referring simply to the Church as an institution here on earth, but to what we might call a state of affairs—that is, a changed condition. Just what might that change be?

Here we might turn to the last book of the New Testament, the much-discussed but also often-misused Book of Revelation, or the Apocalypse of John, as it is known in the Greek tradition. In it, Christ reveals himself as "the Alpha and Omega, the first and the last, the beginning and the end" (Rev 22:13), he who "was dead" but now is "alive forever and ever" (Rev 1:18).

The main purpose of the author of Revelation was to reassure Christians who were suffering persecution and to give them new hope. The book reveals the glorified Christ who is the ruler of the universe, enthroned in glory, in command of heaven and earth. This theme of the *Pantocrator* (literally, "the ruler of all") has been given visual expression in countless icons and mosaics throughout ancient and medieval Christianity; it has illustrated the meaning of Christ's victory over sin, suffering, and death. Back when the earth was considered to be the center of the cosmos, it made great sense to picture the risen and ascended Christ as seated upon or above the clouds, commanding or surveying all that went on below.

Among the most famous are those stemming from the icons ascribed to the fifteenth-century Russian artist Andrei Rublev. In Rublev's icons, we have a graphic expression of the Christ who is, as expressed in the Epistle to the Colossians (1:15ff.), "the image of the invisible God,...the first-born of all creation,...in [whom] all things hold together," the Christ who is the eternal Son of God, or, as St. John the Evangelist describes him in the prologue to his Gospel, the eternal Word of God. This is the Son as God's original image and eternal expression of himself.

Yet we also have Jesus Christ, "born of a woman, born under the law" (Gal 4:4) as St. Paul tells us; in other words, the eternal encapsulated in a human nature and subjected to the constraints of location in space and time. So how can we relate the two, the eternal Son of God and the time-bound son of Mary; the infinite and the limited?

One possibility, inspired by Rublev's icon, is offered by artworks that emphasize the cosmic dimensions of Christ's triumph in terms of unusual geometric patterns enclosing the human figure of Jesus, while he is depicted as seated in his heavenly throne; or again, in those in which he is surrounded by the choirs of angels. Another way would be to think of the way that an artist may produce a very limited number of prints of his or her own original, each copy usually signed and numbered, for example, as "No. 5 of 100," and so on. Might it be possible that Jesus can be seen as the human "print" of God's eternal Word or image? That he can be seen as a "copy" of God that God himself has made? Of course, this is an imperfect analogy, since Jesus isn't a copy but the real, visible manifestation of an invisible reality. But as long as we keep that in mind, it may help us to see how the eternal Son of God and the Jesus of history relate to each other.

There are several reasons for these suggestions. One has to do with the challenge presented by modern science, cosmology in particular, that makes it highly unlikely that we are alone in the universe. And if we are not alone, are we correct in assuming that we are the only creatures to be granted a visit by God in the form of God's own Word or Son? Might it not be that, much like artists today, God has produced at least a limited number of prints or copies of his own image, perhaps each one varying a bit to suit the audience, but each one authenticated or signed by God's Spirit as a copy of the image of the God who contains all things within himself? This, of course, is only a hypothesis, but it is one that needs to be explored if we are to hold to the Church's teaching regarding the universal scope of the redemption while we become more aware of the vast reaches of the universe.

Another response to this challenge is that which was suggested by the Catholic evolutionary scientist Pierre Teilhard de Chardin, who, a few years before his death in 1955, suggested that to accomplish this universe-spanning effect, Christ might be seen as possessing a third, or cosmic, nature in addition to his divine and human natures.[5] This would be in line with Teilhard's earlier (1924) characterization of the Incarnation as a kind of "inoculation" of matter with the "Universal Christ," thus making possible the universe's transformation.[6] In the meantime, unless the scripture scholars decide that the description of Christ in the Epistle to the Colossians as "the image of the invisible God" should not be interpreted quite so literally, we are free to consider the various solutions to this theological challenge. On a more down-to-earth level, we are charged with reproducing the image of Christ in our own selves.

QUESTIONS FOR REFLECTION AND DISCUSSION

1. Why do you think John's Gospel contains no description of the ascension of Christ?
2. Do you find language like "the right hand of God" helpful today? Why or why not?
3. Which do you find more meaningful: the description of the Son as God's image or as God's Word? Give your reasons for your choice.
4. In terms of the whole universe, do you think it likely that God may have produced many self-images or spoken many Words to reveal himself? If so, how do you understand the claim that Jesus is God's only begotten son?

-11-

HE WILL COME AGAIN

...from whence he will come again to judge the living and the dead.
(Apostles' Creed)

*He will come again in glory to judge the living and the dead,
and his kingdom will have no end.*
(Nicene Creed)

The "from whence" in the above phrase in the Apostles' Creed refers to Christ's present state, so here we are entering once more into the realm of time, but now in terms of the future. Here we express our belief that at the end of time, Jesus will return to conduct a final judgment (and sentence) upon human history.

This latter is not exclusively a Christian belief. In some way it was shared by those Jews who believed that God's Messiah would come as a conquering king and judge. And it is still shared by Muslims as well, who, even if they do not believe that Jesus was the Son of God (for them God can have no sons), still revere him as the great prophet whom God will send at the end of the world "to judge the living and the dead." So although the actual identity of the judge may be in dispute, belief in a future judgment is not.

We have to face the fact that the importance of this belief has become greatly diminished during the course of Christian history. It is hard for us today to grasp how seriously the first Christians took it. In many early Christian homes or churches, every Saturday night a vigil of all-night prayer began that ended only on Sunday morning. This was because the Christians hoped that Jesus might return at any time. They assumed that he would probably show up on his day—that is, the Lord's day—and there they would all be, waiting and ready to greet him!

All this may sound a little strange to us today, but is it—really? It may be true that the early Christians misjudged how soon Christ would return and eventually had to begin adjusting to the delay. We can see a shift of outlook in the later epistles of Paul, in the Gospel of Luke, and even more in John, who hardly mentions any final reckoning or judgment. In fact, the Second Epistle of Peter (one of the later New Testament documents to be written) addresses this crisis, which was starting to affect the early Christians when it began to look as if Jesus might not return within their lifetime (2 Pet 3:3–10).

So it has been ever since in the history of Christianity. Periodically new movements, even new sects, would appear claiming that they knew the final judgment would be soon. This especially happened when the year 1000 approached. Such beliefs also sparked a major revivalist movement in the United States back in the 1840s. More recently, such ideas began to circulate during the year 1999—and no doubt will again in 2999 and 3999, and so on, until, quite unexpectedly, the world does come to an end, at least for intelligent life on this planet. And when that happens, we can be sure the judgment will not be a happy one for any of us who contributed in any way to the end of human life on planet earth.

Of course, it can always be pointed out that sooner or later, all life on earth is doomed. A few billion years from now, the sun, which is about halfway through its ten-billion-year lifespan, will go into its predicted red giant stage and swallow up all the inner planets between us and it and will fry everything on earth to a cinder. For that matter, astrophysicists also predict that, as the universe continues to expand from its big bang beginning, life anywhere in the universe will eventually be impossible. And remember, the latest data shows that the rate of this expansion is speeding up rather than slowing down.

Can any of these scientific predictions serve as an excuse for not taking care of the earth that God has given us? Some Christians, predicting the end of the world—or even hoping for it to happen soon—seem to think that taking better care of the earth is not all that important. A similar attitude seems to have occurred among at least some of the early Christians. In St. Paul's Second Epistle to the Thessalonians (3:8–10), we find the apostle complaining about some Christians in that city who were apparently sitting around doing nothing while they waited for the second coming of Jesus. It was this situation that prompted Paul to issue his famous command: "Anyone unwilling to work should not eat" (v. 10).

The implications of this message should be clear for all of us. God gave us this earth as a home for the human race. He seems to have waited at least 100,000 years after humans first appeared before he sent us Jesus, his Word made flesh, to instruct us how to do a much better job of caring for one another; and if we are to care for one another, then we must also care for the earth that is our home. From that perspective, it seems presumptuous to assume that after only 2,000 years God will let us "off the job" so quickly. To compress the cosmic time scale to manageable units, that would be like being hired on a one-year contract and then being told to leave after the first two minutes! Instead, if the parables in the Gospels about those hired to do a job tell us anything, God is going to expect much more from the human race than we have already accomplished. So while science tells us that some day not just the earth, but even the whole universe, will cease to be a home to life, nevertheless, faith tells us that what we accomplish to build up God's kingdom here and now in time will not be lost, but will remain to bear fruit beyond the confines of space and time.

QUESTIONS FOR REFLECTION AND DISCUSSION

1. Some have suggested that Christianity is outdated because the first Christians (and possibly even Jesus, in terms of his human consciousness) thought that the world was about to end. What is your answer to that?
2. Given that the early Christian time perspective was not accurate, what issues may have to be rethought?
3. Given that the world will eventually come to an end, what do you see as the Christian's primary vocation in the world?

Part III

God as Sanctifier

12

THE HOLY SPIRIT

I believe in the Holy Spirit.
(Apostles' Creed)

We believe in the Holy Spirit, the Lord, the giver of life,
who proceeds from the Father and the Son,
who with the Father and the Son is worshiped and glorified,
He who has spoken through the Prophets.
(Nicene Creed)

The third part of the Apostles' Creed simply proclaims, "I believe in the Holy Spirit," and then goes on to list all the effects that flow from the work of the Spirit.

The Nicene Creed, on the other hand, first treats at some length the nature of that Spirit. Actually, this section of the Nicene Creed was made, not at the Council of Nicaea, but later at the First Council of Constantinople in 381, and then only in part. Until that time, most Christians thought of the Spirit simply as God's life-giving power—an *it* rather than a *he* or a *she*, since the Greek word *pneuma* is neuter. However, the Hebrew word for spirit, *ruach* (which also means "wind" or "breath"), happens to be feminine—a *she*. But in the Gospel of John, we find the Spirit called the *Advocate* or *Paraclete*— which in Greek is masculine—a *he*. So the Spirit gradually began to be recognized as a divine *person*, "the Lord, the giver of life," existing from all time, and thus, the Spirit is equal to the Father and the Son, and equally deserving of worship.

through the Son

This theological evolution did not take place without controversy, however. Even today the unfortunate result of that controversy is enshrined in an addition, the so-called *fili-oque* clause, which, in addition to saying the Spirit "proceeds from the Father," adds "and [from] the Son." This later addition to the Nicene Creed was first made by the Spanish Church in 447, but its use was prohibited by Pope Leo III in 809. Nevertheless, the phrase was reintroduced in Rome by Pope Benedict VIII in 1014 and officially added to the Latin version of the Nicene Creed by the Second Council of Lyons in 1274 after a first, but short-lived, attempt was made to heal the break between the East and West. Yet even today the *fili-oque* clause is not accepted by Eastern Orthodox Christians. While some may see this rift to be simply an issue of papal power trumping that of an ecumenical council, actually there is a great deal more at stake. For, in their insistence that the Spirit comes from the Father alone, Orthodox Christians, with their more sophisticated philosophical heritage, were emphasizing a hierarchical distinction between the Father, Son, and Spirit, with the emphasis on the Father, who is the source of all things. The Western Church, with its then current problem of dealing with people recently converted from pagan belief in many gods, instead chose to emphasize the unity of Father, Son, and Spirit, with all equally the one and the same God.

In 1438–45, another attempt was made at the Council of Ferrara-Florence to heal the breach by explaining that the addition really means *through* rather than *from* the Son. The Greek theologians who attended that council accepted that explanation as solving the problem, but when they returned to their homeland they found most people unwilling to accept the new agreement they had made. It seems that their citizens were still outraged by the terrible destruction of their capital, Constantinople, by the crusaders, who, on their way to the Holy Land in 1204, had turned their fury against the Greeks instead.

Surely, there should be a lesson to be learned from this tragedy. Might it not be that—whatever our theological differences, which may have their origin more in philosophical premises than in the scriptures themselves—how we learn to love one another as Christians is, in the end, much more important than how we understand the details of our beliefs? As St. Augustine once urged: "In essentials unity, in nonessentials diversity, but in all things charity." If the exact nature of God is the unfathomable mystery we claim it is, then how can we fail to see that God's Spirit is also mysterious? Whether we see it as "the Spirit of Jesus" (Acts 16:7, Phil 1:19) or, as in John's Gospel, the Paraclete sent to us from the Father and the Son, is it not, in absolute terms, ultimately the same Spirit?

Finally, we need to consider the implications of another phrase added to the Nicene version of our creeds—the part about the Holy Spirit having "spoken through the prophets." We have already alluded to the fact that certain Christians of non-Jewish background found God, as pictured in what we now call the Old Testament, so unlike the God revealed by Jesus, that they tried to repudiate the Old Testament altogether. On the other hand, the growing friction between Christians and Jews caused the latter to repudiate all—Christian claims that the Old Testament prophets had predicted the coming of Jesus, his death, and his resurrection. So obviously, this statement in the Nicene Creed can be seen as a countermeasure against both tendencies.

Today, however, we might see it as pointing to an even broader influence of the Holy Spirit, even among non-Christians, than many Christians are willing to admit. This is not a new idea. In fact, a number of early Church Fathers and theologians believed that God's Spirit was also at work among some of the pagan philosophers even before the time of Christ. Socrates and Plato, in particular, were thought to have been, at least in part, inspired or led to the truth by God, no doubt because of their teachings, above all about the immortality of the soul—something that is not very clear in the Bible, especially in the Old Testament.

So too, in much the same way today, the Second Vatican Council speaks about the influence of the Holy Spirit at work among non-Christians, perhaps even in certain aspects of some of the world's other great religions. The council saw some of these things (even if not all of them) as a preparation for the full reception of the truth revealed in the Gospels. Pope John Paul II, in particular, repeatedly stressed this belief, urging Catholics and all Christians to try to work together with other religions and all people of goodwill for the furthering of peace and the benefit of all humanity.

Finally, we have to consider how the Holy Spirit may be at work in individual lives. In John's Gospel, Jesus tells us that the Spirit, like the wind, "blows where it chooses" (John 3:8). So too in our own lives, God may speak to us in unseen and unexpected ways. For some, the voice of God's Spirit is discovered in the words of others meant especially for them alone. For others it can be discovered, as the Second Vatican Council reminded us, in "the signs of the times." And for still others, it may only become clear in the pains, trials, and errors of life.

Perhaps one thing especially needs to be said. Although we will see it again when we consider our final destiny and the meaning of resurrection, it is altogether necessary that we must understand that the presence of God's Spirit is not some mere extra or an option in our lives. The Bible assures us that God's Spirit is the origin, the source, and the sustenance of all life. The psalmist makes this very clear: Speaking about all living beings, he wrote:

> When you hide your face, they are dismayed;
>> when you take away their breath, they die
>> and return to their dust.
> When you send forth your spirit, they are created;
>> and you renew the face of the ground. (Ps 104:29–30)

So, too, in much the same way, St. Paul tells us that it is God's Holy Spirit that is "bearing witness with our spirit" (Rom 8:16) and is "giving us his Spirit in our hearts as a first installment" (2 Cor 1:22) on the future that awaits us. What Paul is saying is that, as mere humans, we are incomplete beings. Our own spirit is but an aspiration, a potentiality, but—like an empty bag or sack—is one that can never fulfill its destiny on its own. Only God can fill that void. So it seems that God has made us, through the long slow process of evolution, to become not just the rational animal that the ancient philosopher Aristotle described but, through the power of the Spirit who raised Jesus from the dead, coheirs of eternity with Christ.

QUESTIONS FOR REFLECTION AND DISCUSSION

1. How important does it seem to you whether the Spirit is thought of as coming from the Father or from the Father through the Son?

2. Do you think that God's Spirit works in people around the world, despite their different religious beliefs or even sometimes through these other beliefs?

3. How do you see the Holy Spirit operating in your own life?

13

THE HOLY CATHOLIC CHURCH

I believe…in the holy catholic Church.
(Apostles' Creed)

We believe in one holy catholic and apostolic Church.
(Nicene Creed)

Before we get into the issue of what all these adjectives mean or imply, we first have to be clear about what we mean by the word *church*. Of course, here we are talking not about a building, but an organization—an institution, if you will. But even that may be inflating things a bit. The Greek word that appears in the New Testament is *ekklesia*, meaning a "gathering of those who have been called together." The word appears often in the epistles but only twice in the Gospels, both times in Matthew, where it is probably a translation of the Aramaic word *qahal*, which means much the same. Jesus already had an informal gathering during his public ministry, including some seventy-two disciples whom, according to Luke (10:1), he sent out on a mission to help prepare the way. This number may symbolize the list of nations found in the book of Genesis, which, in turn, may simply be Luke's way of emphasizing the universality of Christ's message. But undoubtedly Jesus had many more followers, among whom were a group of women who followed him from Galilee to his final days in Jerusalem.

Nevertheless, it is especially significant that Jesus chose twelve disciples to be his special apostles or emissaries. The number suggests that he was first of all intentionally aiming at a reform of the religion of his own people, who saw themselves as originally constituted of twelve tribes, even though by the time of Jesus their descendants had been already scattered to some degree from their homeland into Europe, North Africa, and all over the Middle East.

So did Jesus intend to found a new religion? Or would it not be more accurate to say that he was intending a reform of his own Jewish faith, which was itself in the process of reaching out with the message of God's promise of salvation to all the nations of the earth? In fact, if we study the New Testament carefully, especially the early history of the Church that we find in the Acts of the Apostles, we will see that the biggest question facing the first Christians was whether or not those who wished to be followers of Jesus had to become Jewish first. According to Luke (see Acts 15), a meeting was held between Paul and some of the original apostles in Jerusalem about the year 50 (a proto-council), and only then was it decided that the "Christians"—as they were by then being called (Acts 11:26)—did not have to become full-fledged Jews with all the special rules that involved.

This does not mean, however, that these early Christians thought of themselves as following a new religion. Instead, they saw themselves as being a continuation of God's chosen people, except that "membership" was now open to all the people on the face of the earth.

This leads us, in turn, to the question of what is meant by the word *catholic*. Today we usually translate this Greek word (*katholikos*) as meaning "universal." But this is not quite accurate. In the Latin, *uni*, when combined with the verb *vertere*, means to "turn into one" or, even more literally, "to pivot around a certain pole or center." In the Roman Catholic mind, this tends to add up to one thing: either you recognize and obey the pope or you're not a Catholic. However, *catholic* in

Luke Timothy Johnson — "being religious means to organize your life around certain experiences + interpretations concerning the meaning of ultimate powers."

the original sense of the word—derived from the Greek words *kata/kath* ("pertaining to") plus *holos* ("the whole")—implies seeing a greater or higher unity, but even while embracing or accepting quite a variety of differences. For example, the great fourth-century bishop St. Cyril of Jerusalem gives four reasons to describe the Church as being catholic: First, the Church has spread all over the earth. Second, it teaches everything we need to know for our salvation. Third, it takes in all classes of people. And fourth, it promotes all forms of virtue and forgives all types of sin (*Catechesis* 18:23). Nevertheless, one can still also say, as it often is said, that another word for *catholic* is *universal*, especially in view of the first item on Cyril's list.

Does this mean that Cyril, as an Eastern Christian patriarch, was ignoring the special position of the Bishop of Rome? It hardly seems likely. In fact, when the Eastern bishops assembled at Chalcedon in 451 to refine the definition of the dual nature of Christ as both divine and human, they had unanimously agreed, after reading a letter sent to them by Pope Leo the Great, that the apostle "Peter has spoken through Leo." By this they did not claim that Leo was necessarily speaking infallibly (it took about another thousand years before the idea of infallibility became more widespread in the West). Because he was the bishop whose post could be traced back to St. Peter's martyrdom in Rome, they were attesting to the fact that Leo, like all of St. Peter's successors, was fulfilling the special role of leadership that was ascribed to the Roman Church back in the second century by St. Irenaeus (bishop of what we now know as Lyons, France), who himself was a disciple of St. Polycarp, bishop of Smyrna, who in turn was initiated into the faith by St. John the apostle.

Next, we have to consider the addition of the words *one* and *apostolic* in the Nicene Creed to the "holy catholic church" in the Apostles' Creed. Here the Nicene Creed echoes St. Paul's proclamation of "one Lord, one faith, one baptism, one God and Father of all" (Eph 4:5–6). Yet, as is evident from the

78

sheer length of St. Irenaeus's long treatise *Against the Heresies*, early Christianity almost from the start was an extremely varied, even divided, movement. Thus it becomes all the more evident that catholic oneness or unity has always been more of a belief or a goal to be achieved than a statement of an accomplished fact. As we have already seen in chapters 4 and 5, there were many different opinions as to *who* Jesus really was, and even where there was more or less agreement on that point, there still was disagreement as to how the Church was to be organized and run.

This, in turn, brings us to what was seen, at the time of the Council of Nicaea, as the most critical historical mark of the authentic Church—namely, that it was founded by or upon the testimony or witness of the apostles. Again, according to St. Irenaeus, each authentic Church was founded either by an apostle or by their successors who inherited their authority. This is why, even today, the World Council of Churches[7] recognizes three ranks of ordained ministry—bishop (*episkopos*), priest (*presbyter*), and deacon (*diakonos*)—as being solidly rooted in the New Testament, even if it doesn't go quite so far as did St. Ignatius of Antioch, who maintained that apart from these three orders, "no church deserves the name."[8]

This is why, in turn, if Christian unity is ever to be achieved, it is probably going to have to involve a new, more fully *ecumenical*—that is, worldwide—council. It will probably have to be one that involves not just the bishops of the Roman and Eastern Catholic Churches, but the participation of *all* the world's bishops and the leaders of *all* the Christian denominations who subscribe to these two creeds. They will need to meet together to forge out a new understanding of what it means to be truly, wholly, and authentically catholic. While Roman Catholics may genuinely believe that their Church contains all the essentials (the meaning of the word *subsists* in Vatican II's Dogmatic Constitution on the Church),[9] it should seem obvious that until an agreement on this point is reached, full and actual catholicity remains more of a dream than a fact.

Nevertheless, if we are to take seriously the prayer of Jesus "that they all may be one," as expressed in the Gospel of John (17:21), then it seems that if Christians are to fulfill God's will, they have no choice but to concentrate on achieving this goal. In a shrinking world where globalization has become a threatening word, this is a big challenge in itself. But despite all our differences, we form *one* human race, we live on a *single* planet, and despite the different names we may use, there really is only *one* God. In other words, we have no realistic choice for harmony and peace in the world unless we take a truly *catholic* view of things—regardless of whether we spell it with a capital C or not. Without this overriding concern for a truly catholic unity, it would seem doubtful that any Christian, much less church organization, can claim to be *holy*—as we shall soon see when we take up the next article of the Apostles' Creed. In Christianity, holiness and wholeness are inescapably linked.

whole

QUESTIONS FOR REFLECTION AND DISCUSSION

1. What is the true meaning of the word *church*? What do you think Jesus really had in mind?
2. What do you see as the implications (especially intellectual, psychological, and spiritual, as well as geographical) of being *catholic*?
3. Considering Jesus' prayer "that all may be one" (John 17:21), what do you think of the ecumenical movement? How far should it go?

Ecumenism

v5 Syncretism, threat of adaptation - loss of power dissolve, degeneration

14

THE COMMUNION
OF SAINTS

I believe…in the communion of saints.
(Apostles' Creed)

One of the curiosities of the Apostles' Creed, in contrast to the Nicene Creed, is that it alone mentions belief in the communion of saints. It appears, however, that this phrase was added to the Western version of this baptismal creed only later on, at the end of the fifth century. Although the phrase has its origin in the East, it is missing from the Greek version of the creeds.

Is it because this particular belief is any less important? One might not think so, but perhaps because of the emphasis on the *oneness* of the Church in the Nicene Creed, the mention of the communion of saints (because, after all, *communion* means the state of unification or sharing together) might be seen as being unnecessary or even a bit redundant.

On the other hand, the term *saints* opens up a number of questions and dimensions to this oneness that we need to explore. This word is used in Paul's epistles to designate *all* members of the Church. This does not mean that every member of the Church is perfect or holy—for even the word *saint*, at least in biblical terms, does not mean what we might first think it does. If it did, life might be easier.

Instead, when the Bible speaks of something being holy or someone being a saint, it means it primarily in the same way as the Hebrew word *kadosh*, which means something or someone that is set apart (by nature or essence, not location) from the rest of the created world—set apart like God himself. Consequently, the opposite of what is holy is not what is evil or depraved but rather what is commonplace, profane, or merely ordinary. Thus, when we speak of the communion of saints, we are not talking about supernatural communication between ourselves and those in the next world. Instead, we are talking about what we are all called to be here and now, simply as members of the Church. In other words, belief in the communion of saints, although it does not exclude those who have gone before us, has to do most of all with our relationship here and now with each other as members of the Church.

So what does this mean in practice? First, it means that we who, according to St. Paul, form the Body of Christ here on earth are intimately linked not only to our head who is the glorified Christ, but also to one another, much as the various parts of our own body are linked to one another. As Paul tells us in his First Epistle to the Corinthians (12:21, 26):

> The eye cannot say to the hand, "I have no need of you," nor again the head to the feet, "I have no need of you."...If one member suffers, all suffer together with it; if one member is honored, all rejoice together with it.

If all this is true, then it also means that it needs to be expressed in our conduct with or toward each other, beginning even with our Sunday worship. It may strike many Christians as odd that there is no direct reference to the rite of sacramental communion in either creed, unlike the explicit mention of baptism in the next article of the Nicene Creed. One reason may be the caution with which the early Christians spoke of this central act of worship, using indirect terms such as "the breaking of the bread" (Acts 2:42, 46), "the Lord's supper" (1 Cor 11:20), the Eucharist (from the Greek *eucharistia*, meaning "thanksgiving"), the *synaxis* (which means "a coming together"), the Divine Liturgy (from the Greek *liturgia*, meaning "the work of the people"), or as became common in the Western Church, the Mass (from the Latin word *missa*, referring to what happened in church after the penitents or the catechumens and others not yet fully instructed in the Christian faith were dismissed). Another reason for the creeds' reticence is that no significant doubts as to the real presence of Christ in this sacrament were raised until the ninth century—some five centuries after the formation of the creed. The main point, however, is that our *communion* or *union together* as Christians is even more fundamental. Without reference to or awareness of our bonds with and obligations toward our fellow Christians; without our consciousness of the presence as well as of the neediness of Christ in our fellow human beings—sacramental communion runs the risk of becoming a hollow ritual. In fact, we can read condemnations of such attitudes and conduct in people who say they believe that we are all one in Christ, and yet, even while professing that belief and partaking in Holy Communion, turn around and kowtow to the rich and neglect the poor (2 Cor 11:17–22; Jas 2:1–9).

All this is not to say that a special bond of unity doesn't also exist between us and those who have passed beyond. The ancient Christian practice of praying to—or better, *through*—the saints is to be commended, as long as it doesn't detract or distract us from the worship that is due only to God.

Add to that, especially, that we should pray for all those who have died and gone before us, especially for those who lived less-than-perfect lives while they were here with us on earth. How their present state, which we tend to think of in terms of the passage of time and have traditionally called *purgatory*, relates to the timeless state that we call eternity is a mystery. Yet this practice of praying for them, attested to in 2 Maccabees 12:28–45 and by inscriptions found on many early

Christian tombs, is still another dimension of what was meant by the communion of saints.

This brings us, finally, to the topic left over from the previous section, where we delayed in our discussion of what the Nicene Creed means when it speaks of the Church as being holy, besides being one, catholic, and apostolic. We cannot avoid this question forever, especially in these days when the Church is being so roundly criticized, and perhaps deservedly so. There is no doubt there have been periods of decline and corruption in the Church, and perhaps this has been one of them. Yet if we look through the annals of Church history, we will find that almost always such declines are counterbalanced or reversed by an upsurge of renewal and increased dedication from others in the Church, often by new movements.

Sometimes these renewals take the form of a reaction, as it did around the age of Constantine, as Christianity, when it became more established, also became worldlier. It was this situation that gave rise to those first monks and nuns, people who fled to the deserts to seek greater separation from the world.

Again, it may take another form, as it did in the Middle Ages, when society became more cosmopolitan and business oriented. In reaction, people like Francis of Assisi and others sought to introduce a more radical way of living within the very midst of ordinary life. They acted as leaven to try to humanize as well as Christianize a society that was becoming ever more obsessed with individual success and wealth.

Then again, at the time of the Protestant and Catholic Reformations—which also happened to be the great era of European expansion and colonization—we find new movements and organizations, such as the Society of Jesus (the Jesuits) founded by St. Ignatius of Loyola. They simultaneously sought to reform the Church from within, to spread the Gospel to foreign lands, and to advance not only Christian but even scientific and human knowledge on all levels, so that (according to the Jesuit motto) "All things [might be] for the honor and glory of God."

Today, we still see all these paths open to us, but especially the last, for *all* Christians, whatever their state in life. The Holy Spirit at work within each of us calls us and equips us to do our own special and, to that extent, irreplaceable part. May we always be awake and listening for that call!

QUESTIONS FOR REFLECTION AND DISCUSSION

1. What was the original meaning of the term *saint* and how would you see it applying to all Christians?
2. What is the difference and the connection between *union* and *communion*? How might this apply to our conduct at Sunday or weekend worship?
3. How do you see the connection between the living and the dead?
4. How would you describe the vocation of the average Christian in today's world?

15

BAPTISM AND FORGIVENESS

I believe…in the forgiveness of sins.
(Apostles' Creed)

We acknowledge one baptism for the forgiveness of sins.
(Nicene Creed)

In its mention of baptism, specifically "one baptism for the forgiveness of sins," the Nicene Creed follows a number of versions of the baptismal creeds found in the Eastern Churches, while the Roman form of the more ancient creed speaks only of the "forgiveness [*remissio* in Latin] of sin," with no mention of baptism. Why this difference? It is hard to say, but we do know that in some places in the early Church, the practice of rebaptism was a hot issue. In North Africa, in particular, the Donatists (who followed the bishop Donatus in his refusal to recognize baptism conferred by clergy who had wavered in the face of the last major persecution) had caused a major schism in the Church there. St. Augustine, for example, lamented the fact that these fellow Christians, whom he called "our brothers," refused to honor the baptism conferred in the Catholic Churches because they regarded the Catholic clergy as too lax and too ready to forgive all kinds of sins.

Today, we have something of a similar situation. Certain Christian groups refuse to accept baptism conferred on infants and children. Others, especially some Pentecostals, insist that infant baptism is a mere formality and that to be a real Christian, one must be "baptized in the Spirit" and thus be "born again." This situation points to a real problem, one that has to do with the meaning not only of baptism, but of all the sacraments. Are they just little ceremonial reminders, or are they actual means of conveying God's grace?

This is where the link to the belief in the forgiveness of sin is crucial. As the Gospels say, "Only God can forgive sin" (Mark 2:7; Luke 5:21). So the linking of baptism to the forgiveness of sin is just another way of saying that it is not the priest who is forgiving sin, but it is God or Christ working through the bishop, or priest.

But if this is the case with baptism, why then baptize only once? We know that in the early Church, most recipients of baptism were adult converts. Back then, the baptizing of babies, who were considered innocent, was relatively rare and still controversial. And so closely linked was baptism to the idea of total conversion, that many people—even Emperor Constantine, who had convened the Council of Nicaea—put off getting baptized until they were lying on their deathbeds. The only alternative, if one had been baptized earlier and then seriously fell or backslid from one's baptismal promises, was to undergo a rigorous discipline of public confession and penance, which was described by some as a second baptism, only not by ordinary (or even blessed) water, but this time by tears.

Eventually the Church relented and allowed this renewal of baptism, which we now call the *sacrament of penance* or of *reconciliation*, to be conferred by a priest standing in for the bishop, and in the privacy of the confessional (now often called the reconciliation room) instead of a church full of onlookers.

Even after the introduction of private confession, however, the assigned penance or penances were still very rigorous. They were usually prescribed according to norms laid down in books called "penitentials"—which served as the medieval equivalents of later manuals on moral theology.

Some penances, such as those usually assigned for the sins of idolatry, apostasy in any form, murder, or adultery, typically amounted to a lifetime of excommunication with a promise of readmission to the sacraments on one's deathbed. It was not a very forgiving Church, at least according to the books.

In practice, the Church was actually often more lenient, and this is where the custom of *indulgences* entered in. The idea is based on the doctrine of the communion of saints as well as the binding and loosing power of the Church. Thus the merits of holy persons might be drawn upon to cancel out the penances assigned to the sinners and less holy ones. Alternatively, one might be offered the chance to engage in some other spiritual exercise, such as going on pilgrimage, engaging in some good work, like almsgiving, or even fighting in a crusade to atone for one's sins. Some of these activities, if one judges by Chaucer's *Canterbury Tales* and by the mayhem committed by many of the crusaders, proved quite unwise. Add to all this the impression, however mistaken, that indulgences were sometimes being sold, and it is not hard to see why, in the sixteenth century, Martin Luther rebelled against the Church as he did.

Aside from the logical problem as to how one can earn "time off" from purgatory for those who have already passed out of this world into eternity, the more immediate problem was, and still is, what is meant by the *remission* of sin. The remission or elimination of a penance or substitution of one penance for another would seem to be completely within the purview of the Church. But *forgiveness* of sin, in the sense of removing the *guilt* involved, is something else. Logically, only the person offended can forgive the guilt. So, although the Church can forgive as far as a sin offends the Christian community, all sin offends God; thus, ultimately, only God can forgive sin in any absolute sense. In some of the Eastern rites of the Catholic Church, this distinction is recognized when a priest may pronounce a sinner officially *absolved* from his or her sin (meaning as far as the Church is concerned), but then prays that

God may forgive that sinner rather than deigning to pronounce that it is so. It is also the understanding in many of these Churches that before one presumes to ask for either the Church's absolution or God's forgiveness, one has gone to the person personally offended to beg his or her forgiveness first.

May it not be said, however, that at the heart of all this is the concern to help Christians live according to the whole meaning of their baptism? Baptism is the foundation and the root of all Christian life. It signifies, and is meant to be, in the words of St. Paul, a "death" (Rom 8:13) of "your old self, corrupt and deluded by its lusts" (Eph 4:22), or as St. Basil the Great put it, "a total break with our former way of life." It is for this reason that, while Luther fumed and rebelled against the corruption of the medieval Church's penitential practices, the really radical reformers, such as Menno Simons and the Anabaptists, believed that the whole theology and practice of the baptism of infants and young children had to be abandoned altogether. For these radicals, baptism always had to be a personal choice. Few other Christians, even among the reformers, were willing to go that far, even if later on, others, like the Baptists in America, did abandon infant baptism.

Still, the root problem remains with us today and will probably continue to do so, as long as human nature remains. The need constantly to renew our baptism—whether we were baptized as an infant, as an adolescent, or even as an adult—is always, to some degree, essential until the day we die. Catholics have long had their parish missions. The Baptists and other born-again Christians have their revival meetings. The religious camp meeting has been a hallowed American tradition since the Great Awakening of the 1840s, and today the weekend retreat movement, although it has had some hard times, is far from dead. Newer, innovative forms of such conversion experiences, such as the *Cursillo* (Spanish for "a short course," that is, in Christian life), TEC (Teens Encounter Christ or, more recently, To Encounter Christ), the Neocatechumenate Way, and a host of other programs, are all attempts to make our baptism more effective in our lives. Clearly there is a continuing need to find still more ways to revive the graces of baptism and the commitment it should entail.

QUESTIONS FOR REFLECTION AND DISCUSSION

1. What is the connection between baptism and the forgiveness of sins through the sacrament of reconciliation or penance? What are the implications of this connection?
2. What is your understanding of the difference among forgiveness of sins, their remission, and doing penance for them? How essential is each element?
3. In your experience, what seems to be the best way of continually renewing the sense of having been baptized?

16

RESURRECTION AND LIFE EVERLASTING

I believe in…the resurrection of the body and life everlasting.
(Apostles' Creed)

*We look for the resurrection of the dead
and the life of the world to come.*
(Nicene Creed)

Where the Apostles' Creed speaks of believing in "the resurrection of the body and life everlasting," the Nicene Creed says that "we look for the resurrection of the dead and the life of the world to come." While many may see this only as a slight rephrasing of exactly the same thing, there are some subtle nuances that deserve note.

For one, where the earlier creed speaks of *belief*, the later one seems to be speaking more of a *hope* or *expectation*. Strictly speaking, we can only believe—in the sense of holding something to be true—in what is *already* the case. For example, we can believe that Christ is risen from the dead, but for our own resurrection, which hasn't happened yet, we can really only hope that we will rise. At this point, nothing seems guaranteed.

Furthermore, there seems to be another difference, if not a discrepancy. During the first few generations of Christianity, the focus, as we see in the Apostles' Creed, appears to be on a *physical* resurrection of the body, which is natural enough, considering belief in Christ's resurrection from the tomb. But there is another reason as well, which has to do with the Middle Eastern, especially the Hebrew, understanding of human nature to begin with. For them, humans were made up, not of body and soul, but rather of a body (the *bashar*), which became a living being (*nephesh*) through the power of the breath or Spirit (*ruach*) of God. In other words, the translation of the Hebrew word *nephesh* as meaning the "soul," which is quite common in our English versions of the Old Testament, is somewhat inaccurate. While it is also a Hebrew way of speaking of one's *self*, to understand it as meaning something like the Greek concept of *psyche* or soul is misleading.

If you want to get a better sense of what the Jews of Christ's time meant by "resurrection," read the famous chapter 37 of Ezekiel—the vision of the valley of the dry bones coming back to life. Yes, it is primarily meant to be a prophecy of the restoration of Israel. But it is also a graphic representation of what resurrection meant to most of the Jews of Jesus' own time.

The result of this very literal understanding, however, was that St. Paul, quite early on in his preaching mission, ran into some difficult problems in his attempts to get this idea across. Where Jews and some other Middle Eastern people could imagine life after death only in terms of bodies rising from the grave, the Greeks and quite a few other peoples found this idea rather grotesque, preferring to place their hopes in the idea of a naturally immortal, spiritual soul. This certainly seems to be the situation described by St. Luke in Acts 17:31–33. As a result, St. Paul appears to have gradually altered his approach, describing the resurrection in terms of a "spiritual body" that is altogether unlike the mortal or physical body that is buried in the grave (see 1 Cor 15:44). While there is a certain continuity between the two, there is still a world of difference—in fact, according to Paul, as much as there is between the earth and the stars (which back then were thought to be in a whole world apart).

While the Apostles' Creed mirrors the more ancient Hebrew way of thinking and still speaks in terms of "the resurrection of the body," the Nicene Creed, with its more sophisticated Greek and philosophical way of expressing things, says "resurrection of the dead." So while we can continue to believe that the miraculous resurrection of Christ took place as a visible physical reality, still, it was meant to serve as a symbol of a more lasting spiritual state. At least this is what the later creed of Nicaea-Constantinople seems to mirror in this more refined wording of what resurrection might mean for us.

Yet, is even this more-nuanced understanding believable in this day and age? Oddly enough, perhaps even more so than before. Today, when science tells us that matter is really only frozen energy or energy that has been congealed into certain fixed patterns, it is increasingly difficult to divide the world into separate realms, one strictly material in nature, and another entirely spiritual. Instead, the two exist only in relation to each other—or as Einstein's famous equation (when reversed) implies, energy is liberated matter traveling at the speed of light. So if we are, as the great seventh-century Greek theologian St. Maximus the Confessor put it, the creation of what he called "the divine energies," then might not we conclude that our eternal destiny is to be reunited with that source of divine life and light?

What then are "life everlasting" and "the world to come"? Are these merely figures of speech, similar to the phrase "new heavens and a new earth," as found in the prophet Isaiah (65:17), in the Second Epistle of Peter (3:13), and in Revelation (21:1)? In view of what we now know about our universe, it seems unlikely. If you will recall, when we were discussing God as Creator, we mentioned that as far as science can tell us, the material universe, made up of energy and matter (or more accurately, energy becoming matter), had its origin some 13.7 billion years ago in what is generally referred to as the big bang. Until just a few years ago, some cosmologists thought that eventually the big bang might run out of steam and collapse back into what was called the big crunch—resulting in another big bang and so on, over and over again, something like a cosmic reciprocating engine. In such a scenario, there would literally be a whole succession of "new heavens" and "new earths."

The latest findings by astronomers have pretty much quashed such pipe dreams, however. Not only is the big bang continuing to expand, but as of late—that is to say during the past few billion years—it even seems to be speeding up! Eventually the universe that we know seems to be destined to become a completely fragmented shell devoid of life—cold dead cinders of burned out stars and other cosmic rubble. What this means for humanity or any other living creature in the universe is that either we evolve into a higher, more spiritual level of existence, or else nothing much of significance is likely to survive in the far future.

Of course, there are still dreamers among the scientists, especially among the mathematicians who are free to ignore all the observations and other experiments and simply play with numbers. These speculate as to how there might be other parallel universes out there that we can never see or that may still blossom like leaves in spring from a parent entity they like to call a "multiverse." (One wonders how putting faith in such speculations is any different from believing in God!) Yet if these other universes have no connection to ours, it also means that, even if something created might always continue to exist, still the whole process of evolution that took place on our planet eventually turns out to be a dead end. Perhaps this is entertaining to God while it lasts, but it is without any hope or promise for us mere humans.

This is why, at least it seems to me, the Christian faith is so important. Christ is, for us, not only "the image of the invisible God" (Col 1:15), but he is also the guarantee that all that has happened on this tiny rock spinning in space is of great importance to his Father. Christ means to see to it that all of us who are willing to be transformed by his Spirit will share God's life with him for all eternity. For it is then, as St. Paul tells us, that all suffering and death shall be overcome, and Christ shall return all creation to the Father "so that God may be all in all" (1 Cor 15:28).

Amen! So be it!

QUESTIONS FOR REFLECTION AND DISCUSSION

1. What was the difference between biblical and Greek philosophical ideas of immortality?
2. Do you see any significant difference between the statements about the future resurrection in the two creeds? What might this indicate to you?
3. Do present scientific ideas about the future of the universe appear to support or, to the contrary, threaten Christian beliefs?

Afterword

FAITH AND BELIEF

Some years ago, the American religious scholar and theologian Wilfred Cantwell Smith wrote a lengthy book titled *Faith and Belief*,[10] which, had it been written in a less scholarly form, might have saved many people much anguish and suffering. In it, Smith pointed out that in English we have two different words—*faith* and *belief*—to describe quite different aspects of the one term generally used in both the Old and the New Testaments: in Hebrew this word is *emunah*; and in Greek, *pistis*.

Other than taking advantage of what is explicit in his book's title, Smith's analysis was hardly new or groundbreaking. In fact, it echoes that important voice of tradition who spoke at that very time when the Nicene Creed was first completed, St. Cyril of Jerusalem.

> The one word *faith* can have two meanings. One kind of faith concerns doctrines. It involves the soul's ascent to and acceptance of some particular matter....The other kind of faith is given by Christ by means of a special grace....This kind of faith, given by the Spirit as a special favor, is not confined to doctrinal matters, for it produces effects beyond any human capability. If a man who has this kind of faith says to this mountain, "move from here to there," it will move.[11]

hope

96

As Smith kept pointing out, however, we have, at least in English, two words to try to describe these two different yet related aspects of religion. The confusion, and for some the tragedy, is that we have so often failed to take advantage of these two different words in order to explore what is really going on in our spiritual life and its development.

According to Smith, *faith*, at least in the sense of that word as it is generally used in the Gospels, is a fundamental trust, or, as Cyril put it, that grace or power to move mountains. *Belief*, on the other hand, involves the ability of the mind or intellect to grasp and accept or assent not just to the words of the creeds but, more importantly, to the apostolic *kerygma* or message that Jesus is—and, risen from the dead, forever remains—the Christ, the true Son, the very Word, of God.

The medieval scholastic theologians, perhaps more than any other group of persons in Christian history, dedicated their efforts to reconciling faith and reason. They also made some careful distinctions when it came to understanding what was, or might be, meant by the single Latin word *fides* or, as we generally translate it, *faith*. First, or most fundamentally, there was that *faith* or basic *trust* in God or in himself that Jesus sought in those who asked for his help, as described in the Gospels. For example, in Mark's Gospel, Jesus asks the father of the epileptic boy if he believed or had faith, and the father answers, "I believe; help my unbelief" (9:24, NRSV); in the Jerusalem and New Jerusalem Bibles, his reply is perhaps more accurately (at least according to Smith's understanding) given as, "I have faith; help my lack of faith."

Then too, the medieval theologians spoke of a *fides qua* or "faith by or through which" such wonders could be accomplished, which, in turn, corresponds to what St. Cyril had described as the kind of faith (or again perhaps we'd say "trust") that can move mountains.

Finally, and only then, did the medieval theologians speak about *fides quod* or "faith that" a certain item of belief is in fact true—in other words, *belief* as we generally understand

cf William James – The Will to Believe

that word today, despite the fact that (as Smith pointed out) this English word is based on the Germanic root *lieb*, which means "love," and which, in early English, had the connotation of giving one's allegiance. not to some fact or truth, but to some person or ideal. Thus, even when understood in this third sense, which corresponds to St. Cyril's earlier description of the kind of faith by which we accept the articles of the creed, the emphasis was initially on the heart more than on the head or intellect. Or again, as we might put it in today's way of speaking, faith is more an affair of the heart, while belief tends more to involve the intellect. In other words, in this more basic sense faith is more a psychological instinct or drive, while belief or our beliefs represent our attempts to account, in our mind, for this attitude.

The importance of these distinctions cannot, I think, be ignored, much less overrated. For example, recently, some thirty years since the publication of Smith's book, the world was shocked when it was revealed that Mother Teresa, the missionary saint of Calcutta, had suffered agonies of doubt through most of her lifetime. Many wondered, How could this be? How could she have devoted her life to serving the poor in whom she claimed to see Christ, when, for example, she doubted, among other things, whether or not they actually possessed souls that needed saving? How could she have gone on like this? One outspoken atheist (Christopher Hitchens), who had already publicly berated her for her conservative views which he saw as prolonging human misery rather than eliminating it, was quick to denounce her as a pious fraud or hypocrite. And he was not the only one to display such outrage or incomprehension.

The fact is that deep in the history of Christian mysticism, indeed, in the dynamics of human spirituality in general, there has long been the recognition of the fact that our ideas about God are generally, and in the end woefully, inadequate. We already alluded to this fact in the very first chapter of this book, which dealt with our belief in God. What was

not discussed at any length was the fact that the way of analogy—that is, of positive theology, in which divine realities are
discussed in terms comparing them to more earthly things
(for example, God described as Our Father or a Heavenly
King)—will eventually or even inevitably, if we progress far
enough in the spiritual life, become inadequate. Such
approaches are apt to be replaced by what the Greek theologians called the *apophatic* way of negative theology, which recognizes that the reality of God ("the God beyond God," to
quote the medieval mystic Meister Eckhart) is far beyond all
human imagining or intellectual ideas and conceptions. It is
the failure to recognize this or, in the case of Mother Teresa,
the failure of spiritual advisors or directors to point this out
(thank God, she finally did find one who understood what
was going on with her), that can cause so much unnecessary
suffering.

Nevertheless, some of this suffering *is* necessary. It is
part of the growing pains of spiritual development, especially
if one lives long enough and is forced, whether one likes it or
not, to advance toward spiritual maturity. We may stubbornly
resist this harrowing of the soul, but in resisting, we will only
increase the growing pains. *Acceptance, surrender*

At the same time, such growth in faith, whether it begins
with simple belief or even just the ability to believe, is the
result of a special gift or grace. One may argue or reason as
much as one might, but faith, in this sense of belief, cannot be
forced, either on oneself or on someone else. It is and, indeed,
must remain the result of the individual's own free decision.

Nevertheless, it must be understood that this decision
can only be made in response to an invitation, or a "marriage
proposal" made by God. In this way, faith becomes a *commitment* made by us in which we are empowered or privileged to
share in the life, and to some limited extent, in the knowledge
and consciousness, of God himself.

Yet here too we must be careful. Just as one cannot, at
least wisely, marry someone for their money, or their prestige,

Via negativa

or even simply for their looks, in much the same way the choice of a "faith"—at least in the sense of a set of beliefs—should not be made on the basis of the attractions or benefits being offered, even if one of those benefits is the promise of eternal life. Instead, any true commitment to God, if God is to be approached as God, must be "for better or for worse." Anything less is merely self-serving—understandable to begin with, but in the end self-defeating. This is why, in the language of the spiritual masters, those who advance in true holiness can expect to be tested, both by a "night of the senses"—that is to say, by a diminution of the feelings and consolations that often accompany prayer—and ultimately by a "dark night of the spirit," in which the apparent certainty of our various beliefs may be shaken, as were Mother Teresa's. It is only through such a harrowing or winnowing process that our faith can be purified of the egocentrism that remains as a barrier between ourselves and God. It is this same barrier of self-centeredness that was so radically addressed by the Buddha some twenty-five centuries ago, in fact, addressed in so radical a form that its apophatic approach to the ultimate reality is often mistaken for or misnamed atheism.

I believe, however, that there is something else at work here as well. It is what most of all separates our times from those in which Christianity first took shape, as well as from those in which it was still in its ascendancy, the supposed "Age of Faith." Ours, it would seem, is not just a dark night but a dark *age* of faith, one in which the very foundations of Christianity have been shaken, not so much, as is supposed, by science and reason, as by the conceit enshrined in the motto that "man [i.e., ourselves] is the measure of all things." It is this belief, not reason or logic, that has turned the world of faith upside down.

What seems even more ironic is that this new humanity-centered belief came about on the heels of the world-shaking discovery that we no longer could consider ourselves as being at the physical center of the universe. It hardly takes a psychoanalyst to suggest that what humanity collectively did was to substitute the belief that the human race was God's special creation—for which the rest of creation exists—with the still more self-centered belief that we alone can determine the meaning, if not the whole future course, of the universe.

All this suggests that faith, at least in our age, cannot or should not be measured merely in terms of conformity to traditional Christian beliefs. These beliefs can only really be understood by means of a critical reassessment of their historical foundations—such as, for example, an understanding of the political and cultural factors that influenced the outcome of the Council of Nicaea. In contrast, *faith*, in the most radical sense of the word—that is, in the gospel sense of a loving trust in God—can only be defined in terms of, or result from, what theologian Paul Tillich called "ultimate concern," providing that this "ultimate" is something much greater than just ourselves.

In other words, what is needed in this faithless world is not a forced or attempted return to unquestioned conformity to traditional formulations of belief but instead, at least to begin with, a new Copernican revolution in our minds to accompany that which dethroned us (scientifically speaking) from imagining we were at the center of God's universe. I believe that it is only when we truly open ourselves in this way that we can truly regain faith in the most authentic gospel sense of that word. And as for the various beliefs that are enshrined in our creeds in order to express that faith, they will, in time, become better understood—perhaps with new and, as we have seen, even more surprising ramifications.

NOTES

1. Cyril of Jerusalem, *Cat. 5, De fide et symbolo*, 12, in *Patrologia Graeca* 33, 518–19, available at http://www.cross roadsinitiative.com/library_article/283/Two_Kinds_of_Faith __St._Cyril_of_Jerusalem.html.

2. Pope John Paul II, *Evangelium Vitae* (*The Gospel of Life*), 3, §§ 60, 61; available at http://www.vatican.va/edocs /ENG0141/__PQ.HTM.

3. Plotinus, *Enneads* VI: 8, 16; available at http://classics. mit.edu/Plotinus/enneads.6.sixth.html; emphasis mine.

4. Thomas Aquinas, *Compendium of Theology*, trans. Cyril Vollert, SJ (St. Louis: B. Herder Book Co., 1947), 216.

5. Pierre Teilhard de Chardin, "A Sequel to the Problem of Human Origins: The Plurality of Inhabited Worlds," in *Christianity and Evolution*, trans. René Hague (London: Collins, 1971), 236.

6. Pierre Teilhard de Chardin, "My Universe," in *Science and Christ*, trans. René Hague (New York: Harper & Row, 1965), 61.

7. World Council of Churches, "Baptism, Eucharist, and Ministry," Faith and Order Paper No. 111, citation at Ministry III:19. The paper in its entirety is available at http://www.oik oumene.org/en/resources/documents/wcc-commissions/ faith-and-order-commission/i-unity-the-church-and-its-mis sion/baptism-eucharist-and-ministry-faith-and-order-paper- no-111-the-lima-text/baptism-eucharist-and-ministry.html.

8. Ignatius of Antioch, "Epistle to the Trallians," in *The Epistles of St. Clement of Rome and St. Ignatius of Antioch*, trans.

James A. Kleist, SJ, Ancient Christian Writers (Westminster, MD: Newman Press, 1947), 76.

9. Second Vatican Council, *Lumen Gentium* §8, available at http://www.vatican.va/archive/hist_councils/ii_vatican_council/documents/vat-ii_const_19641121_lumen-gentium_en.html.

10. Wilfred Cantwell Smith, *Faith and Belief: The Difference Between Them* (Princeton, NJ: Princeton University Press, 1979).

11. Cyril of Jerusalem, *Cat. 5, De fide et symbolo*, 10–11.

[handwritten annotations:]

one I thing

at Resurrection – exaltation movement

Christology's backward movement – Raymond Brown

70 Mark – at Baptism (adopted) – Son y God – power

85–90 Mt, Lk – at conception = HS annunciation

95 Jn – eternal, pre-existence, logos

INDEX

1 Thess.